Wilderness Canoe Tripping

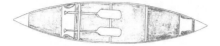

Wilderness Canoe Tripping

Bill Hosford

Ecopress

An Imprint of Finney Company

Lakeville, Minnesota

Notice to the Reader
Every effort was made to make this book as accurate
and up-to-date as possible. However, there are no
warranties, expressed or implied, that the information
is suitable to any particular purpose. The author and
publisher assume no responsibilities.

ISBN: 978-1-893272-14-9

Designed by Angela Wix
Edited by Lindsey Cunneen
Illustrations by Bill Hosford

Ecopress
An Imprint of Finney Company
8075 215th Street West
Lakeville, Minnesota 55044
www.finneyco.com

1 3 5 7 9 10 8 6 4 2
Printed in the United States of America

Preface

This book started as a list of things to be packed for a canoe trip, as a reminder to myself and to help newcomers. A food list was added for shopping and packing. Then some important *do*s and *don't*s were added to the list of food and gear. Finally I decided to expand the whole thing into a book. Many of the ideas came from early trips with Bob Kadlec.

As an engineer, my view of the world is somewhat mathematical and I have allowed this aspect to creep into the writing. My excuse for this is that there are many other engineers who enjoy the wilderness, and I know of no books on canoeing that have any quantitative treatments of the subject. On the other hand I realize that most people aren't comfortable with mathematics, so I've tried to summarize all of the numerical arguments for the innumerate.

True wilderness is something that few people ever experience. A canoe allows one to get away from the civilized world, into otherwise inaccessible places. Two portages are usually sufficient to elude even the most ambitious motorboater. Life takes on different values and requires different attitudes and behavior when the nearest help is days away. One walks more carefully to avoid a sprained ankle. One pays more attention to protecting food and clothes from becoming wet or lost. Life is not so hurried as it is in "civilization." Periods of relaxation at the end of the day seem more precious. Food is more appetizing in the wild. One should be able to enjoy the adventure while avoiding some of the pitfalls into which the neophyte may fall.

This book is not intended as a primer on paddling techniques. Other books do that better. It is intended only as a guide to enjoying the wilderness experience. I have learned much from those with whom I've paddled. In addition to Bob Kadlec, I am especially indebted to George Brooks and my daughter, Jean. An incomplete list of other compatriots with whom I've paddled include: John Stirling, Ed Mooney, Tom Brady, Dennis Kreuger, Kelli Kadlec, Dave Hammer, Wendell Heers, Brymer Williams, Bill McDougald, Johan Nyquist, Fred Woman, Rane Curl, George Benson, Bob Forsburg, Teddy Nelson, George Quarterer, Peter Parker, Red Berensen, Dick and Brian Flinn, Peg, Jon, Ken and Thad Hosford, Kathy, Debbie, Jon and Chris Kadlec, Finis Carlton, Wayne Jones, Alex Graf, Keith Bowman, Ed Marshall, Bob Bignell, Rob Butler, Deb Percival, Mary and Jan Edick, Blair and Graham Richardson, Ian and Dave Malcolm, Marshall Austin, Alan Jacobs, Steve Catlin, Mary and Dan Crouch, Steve Wright, Peggy Hart, Hal Estry, as well as Black Feather and Nahanni River Adventures.

Bob Bignell and Tom Buhr made helpful suggestions. I particularly wish to thank my wife, Peg, and my daughter, Jean, for suggestions. I also wish to thank my niece, Allison, for editing the manuscript.

Contents

Trip Planning

*The arctic explorer Vilhjalmur Stefansson said
that most "adventures" are the result of one of two things:
bad judgment or lack of knowledge.*

Winter months

It's fun to plan a spring or summer trip during the winter months. It's a time when one can: decide where to go, get gear together, plan meals, dry food, and select a party.

Selecting a party

When selecting the people for a wilderness canoeing expedition, I believe that personality is more important than wilderness skills. I try to guess how a potential group member might react after three days of continuous rain or after a two-mile portage finding that they have gone the wrong way and must retrace their steps. I try to guess whether they might grouse about everything or joke about the situation. Nothing can ruin a trip more than a complainer, a worrywart, or someone who withdraws into himself. Then there are those who, like horses, bolt for the barn when they sense a ride is half over. They tend to make every effort to complete an otherwise leisurely canoe trip as rapidly as possible. Of course, if a durable personality is combined with canoeing and camping experience, so much the better. A willing person can quickly learn basic camping and paddling skills. Woods savvy is as important as river skill. The ability to swim is extremely important. Paddling with one's spouse may endanger a marriage. The problem is that one tends to be much less tolerant of a spouse's shortcomings than those of other people.

Finding people who have time for a two or three-week trip is often difficult. In organizing a party, there is a point when each member must make a firm commitment. Each canoe needs two people—not one or three. Often it is impossible to locate an additional person one or two days before departure.

Some people firmly believe that every expedition should have an accepted leader, with military-type control. I, however, prefer trips that are more loosely organized, with decisions being made by general consensus. As a trip progresses, different people will emerge as leaders in different areas of concern: cooking, selecting camping sites, finding portage trails, etc. For me, a canoe trip is a vacation and should not be organized like a military operation.

Deciding where to go

Planning a trip is an activity that can entertain one for hours, days, and weeks through the winter months. Considerations include deciding whether the trip should be a quiet time in the bush or an adventure, whether it should be primarily a fishing trip or not. Other considerations are how much time is available and how much experience the party has.

The time of year will dictate whether some trips are possible. In the early spring, there is usually enough water to paddle streams that would be impassable later in the year, but large rivers may have too much water to be enjoyable. Portage trails may be flooded.

No riverbanks may be suitable for camping and it may be difficult to find dry places to camp. It would be ideal to find the window between the breakup of ice and the first black fly hatch. Occasionally I have succeeded, but more often, I have not.

In the summer, small streams may have too little water and large rivers are likely to have more rock banks for easy walking and camping. Black flies are not as bad in August and the mosquito population is on the decline.

Avoiding green (park) areas on the map increases the chances of experiencing true wilderness as you avoid meeting other parties. One can avoid motorboats only after making two portages and even then there may be fly-in fishing camps.

Maps

Topographical maps for all of Canada are available on the scale of 1:1,000,000 (approximately 1 inch = 16 miles or 25 km) and 1:250,000 (1 inch = approximately 4 miles or 6 km). For much of Canada there are also maps on a scale of 1:50,000 (1 inch = approximately 0.8 miles or 1.25 km).

Topographical maps of the U.S. are available on a 15-minute series (1:50,000) as well as the 1: 250,000 series. They can be obtained from the U.S. Department of the Interior, U.S. Geological Survey at http://topomaps.usgs.gov/index.html. Free indexes for each series are available.

Special maps are available of areas of interest to canoeists. Among these are: Algonquin Park, Nahanni River, Wabakimi, Boundary Waters, Quetico, Spanish River, and Pukaskwa Parks.

When I first started paddling in the Ontario wilderness in the early 1960s, there were no trip sheets available. We had only topographical maps, which gave us the feeling of real exploration. Even today, I feel ambivalent about using other people's trip sheets.

Required time

Maps can be used to estimate the distance to be paddled. Hints on how to account for the tortuous river courses may be found in Appendix 1. Then one must decide what distance can be paddled in a day. If the group can get started on the river by 9:30 a.m. and paddles until 5 p.m. with an hour break for lunch, that amounts to six and a half hours of paddling. For flat water, it is reasonable to assume a speed of 3 mph (5 kmph) if there is no headwind. Current can add to the speed. This works out to about 20 miles or 30 km.

Time must be recalculated if portages are expected. A half an hour should be allotted to loading and unloading. An hour should be allotted for two carries (three walking trips) per portage. The result is that a one-mile portage takes at least an hour and a half. More time is required if the trail is not in good shape. A conservative estimate for the distance to cover is 12 miles (20 km) in a day. The number of paddling days can be estimated by this procedure. For a long trip, a layover day or a day of hiking may be desired. Of course it is wise to allow an extra day (or even two for longer trips) just in case wind or rain forces you to remain in camp. Twice I've spent rainy, windy days in tents (once on the Horton, Northwest Territories, and once on the Thelon, Nunavut). One year the winds on Black Lake, Saskatchwan, were so strong that we had to spend two nights at the last campsite. Several times I've encountered very large waves on Lake Superior that made us head to shore by 2 o'clock in the afternoon.

When plans involve using airplanes to get to the starting place or to get out at the end, allowance should be made for delays caused by weather-grounded planes. Forest fires can delay planes because available planes are required to ferry firefighters and supplies.

Transportation

For some trips it may be possible to drive to the put-in point and leave a car at the take-out point, or to use a railroad train for one or both legs. Often a train will let you off where the tracks cross a river that you want to paddle. More inaccessible locales will require flying. Floatplanes can be hired to drop you off on a lake or river at the start of a trip or to pick you up at the end.

Carrying canoes on a car

A number of cartop carriers are suitable for canoes, ranging from fixed carriers to foam pads. In the past, it was possible to fasten lines to rain gutters, but today few cars have rain gutters. Ropes can be passed through open windows and held fast by shutting the windows.

A common mistake is to position the canoe so that lines from the stern and bow pull the canoe in the same direction. If the canoe slips, both lines slacken.

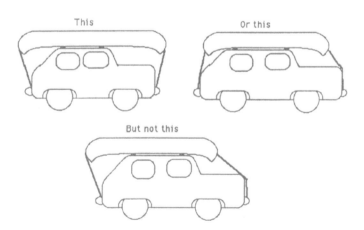

This

Or this

But not this

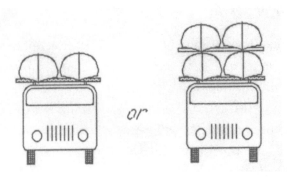

Two canoes can be carried side by side if the carrier is extended with a six-foot plank. Three or even four canoes can be carried by resting lateral bars on top of the two lower canoes. A rigger's knot (Appendix 3) can be used to make the canoes fast.

Tree line on the Horton River, Northwest Territories.

Gear

Most men are incapable of reaching the wilderness,
no matter how hard they try. They thrust before them the
destructive shockwave of civilization, so that any place at
which they arrive—however remote and untrammeled—
is spoiled by their presence, spoiled at the very instant of their arrival.
—Peter Browning in *The Last Wilderness*

The Latin word for baggage is *impedimenta.* Certainly baggage is an impediment on portages. The temptation to take too much must be resisted. One doesn't need all of the comforts of home. Gear may be broken down into three groups: personal things, equipment for each canoe, and items common to the whole group.

Kinds of packs

There are various types of packs. Frame packs designed for backpacking are suitable if the frames are not too long. It is difficult to fit three or four long frame packs into a canoe. Internal frame packs are preferable. Duluth packs, which are soft packs made from canvas and have leather straps, are the traditional packs of Minnesota and Northern Ontario. Wicker baskets are traditional in Maine. A tumpline allows much of the weight to be transferred to the

Last two trees on the Horton River, Northwest Territories.

forehead. Those who have mastered tumplines swear by them. Today there are rubberized waterproof packs that ensure dryness.

Some expeditions carry food in large wooden boxes called wanigans. I have never used a wanigan and the thought of carrying one on a long portage gives me nightmares. I like packing gear into 30-gallon drums, which fit into the canoe and can accommodate a carrying harness. They can be tied into the canoe in such a way as to provide buoyancy in case of swamping. A side benefit is that they can be used as stools at camp. The company Trailhead[1] sells drums with harnesses. Drums can be purchased at a considerably lower price from a commercial supply house.[2] A 30-gallon plastic drum weighs 7 lbs, 4 oz, and a harness weighs 1lb, 4 oz.

Whatever packs are used, it is imperative that they can be carried on the back, rather than in the hands. Duffel bags should not be taken!

---

1   Trailhead—1960 Scott Street, Ottawa, ONT K1Z, 8L8 Canada; (613) 722-4229.
2   For example, Rubbermaid Consolidated Plastics—8181 Darrow Road, Twinsburg, OH 44087; (216) 425-3900.

Personal gear

Personal gear includes what you wear and what is in your personal pack. What to take depends on personal preference. However you should keep in mind that everything, including food and group items, must be carried. A limit of 40 to 45 pounds of packed personal gear is suggested. The list below shows how I have used my weight limit on recent trips. Others may choose to take different things.

Item	No	wt (oz)	wt (g)
hat	1	4.0	100
shirt (light weight/long sleeve)	1	8.5	240
trousers	1	20.0	570
socks (wool)	1 pair	5.0	140
belt	1	5.0	140
compass	1	1.8	50
toilet paper package	1	0.3	10
knee pads	1 pair	4.0	110
personal flotation device	1	16.0	460
T-shirt	1	5.5	160
underdrawers	1	3.0	90
handkerchief	1	0.5	10
sneakers	1	36.0	1020
watch	1	2.0	60
knife (Swiss army)	1	4.0	110
eyeglasses	1	2.0	60
matches	2	0.5	10
Total weight: 7 lb, 5.5 oz (3.34 kg)			

The compass is essential and it should be set for the appropriate magnetic declination. See Appendix 2. The knife and supply of waterproof matches are for emergency. If it's a cold day I will wear more and there will be correspondingly less in my personal pack. Assuming an eight-day trip and a warm day, the clothing and personal gear in my pack will consist of:

Item	No	wt (oz)	wt (g)
wool socks	3 pairs	7.0	200
handkerchiefs	3	1.5	40
shirt (light weight/long sleeve)	1	8.5	240
T-shirts	2	16.5	470
poly-pro pullover	1	16.0	450
trousers	1	20.0	570
filleting knife and sheath	1	13.5	380
extra cup	1	7.0	200
toiletry bag containing soap (hotel size)	1	1.0	30
very small towel	1	3.0	90
toothbrush, paste & floss	1	1.0	80
swimming suit	1	3.0	90
book	1	22.0	630
wallet & car keys	1	3.0	90
sewing kit	1	2.0	60
sleeping bag	1	60.0	1700
some surprise	1	16.0	540
playing cards	1 pack	3.0	90
dry sneakers	1	36.0	1820
underdrawers	3	9.0	260
long underwear	1	7.5	210
shirt (heavy flannel)	1	16.0	450
windbreaker	1	13.0	370
flash light (2 C cells)	1	4.5	130
bayonet & sheath	1	14.0	400
spare eyeglasses	1	2.0	60
toilet paper (300 squares)	1	1.8	50
fishing gear tackle box	1	6.0	170
collapsible pole & reel	1	20.0	570

long nose pliers	1	5.0	140
cigarette lighter	2	1.4	40
water filter	1	32.0	910
garbage bags	2	4.0	100
sleeping pad	1	43.0	1220
pack weight	1	88.0	2500
pee bottle	1	2.0	60
Total weight: 38 lbs, 9 oz (15.4 kg)			

In addition I have a small daypack with:

Item	No	wt (oz)	wt (g)
sun glasses	1	2.0	60
rain gear	1	22.0	630
Sierra cup	1	3.0	90
watercolor box	1	7.0	200
watercolor paper	2	30.0	850
brushes	several	1.5	40
water bottle	1	6.0	170
trowel	1	16.0	450
head net	1	2.0	60
camera	1	8.0	230
bug repellent	1	2.0	50
fork & spoon	1 each	2.5	70
map bag w/ maps	1	3.0	90
pencil & notebook	1	2.0	60
sunburn lotion	1	3.0	90
Total weight: 6 lbs, 14 oz (3.1 kg)			

Most people will not want to carry watercolor supplies and a bayonet. And some will want more reading material, some tobacco, or a video camera. Any alcohol should be considered personal gear. Everyone should carry matches or a cigarette lighter, a compass, and a knife. My Swiss army knife has scissors that I find almost indispensable. And a baggie of toilet paper takes up almost no room.

In choosing a PFD (personal flotation device), remember that the safest life jacket is one the canoeist is most likely to keep wearing and this is usually the one that is most comfortable.

Some neophytes wonder if a sleeping pad or mattress is necessary. The main function of a sleeping pad or mattress is insulation. The portion of the sleeping bag under the body is compressed so it offers little insulation from the cold ground. A pad or mattress offers this needed insulation as well as comfort. Air mattresses are comfortable but sometimes leak. Closed cell foams provide good insulation and don't leak, but they aren't as comfortable as an air mattress and they don't roll up tightly for packing. A good compromise is a self-inflating open-cell foam pad.

The sleeping bag is one of the most important items. Both synthetic and down-filled bags provide excellent insulation. They give basically the same insulation for the same weight, but each has its advantages and disadvantages. Down-filled bags can be compressed into much less space so they are easier to pack. Larger foam-filled bags usually have to be tied onto the outside of the pack. On the other hand, a wet foam-filled bag offers more insulation than a wet down bag. One way of ensuring a dry sleeping bag is to pack it inside of a cloth bag, which can easily be slipped into a waterproof plastic bag. This in turn can be put into another cloth bag to prevent the plastic bag from tearing.

There is the question of how heavy a sleeping bag is needed. The temptation is to buy "the best" and to equate "the best" with the one rated for the lowest temperature. Most of us canoe in the spring or summer when 0°F is less likely than 90°F, so very low temperature ratings are of little importance. On hot nights, the extra insulation is downright uncomfortable. A bag that unzips at the bottom as well as the top allows one to remain cooler on those extra warm nights. A pillow can be made by filling the sleeping bag's stuff bag with soft clothing.

Birches.

I have recently succumbed to taking a light folding camp chair that I use for painting and relaxation. My bayonet is for splitting wood, digging fire pits, and poop pits. Otherwise, a trowel should be carried. The flashlight isn't necessary on late spring and early summer trips because the sun sets so late. The garbage bag is for covering the pack at night to protect it from rain and dew. My sewing kit consists of a needle, thread, a small device for threading the needle, four buttons, and four safety pins in a small tin.

I usually bring a little surprise for the party—not necessary but often fun. A few examples of surprises are: pistachio nuts, a bottle of wine, a small watermelon, neckties for men to wear at dinner, and a loaf of French bread.

Clothing

I wear high sneakers in the bush. Most people, however, prefer hiking boots, which offer more foot protection and support than sneakers. Sneakers dry faster and are lighter. On the one trip that I wore boots, my canoe swamped and I found swimming difficult with boots. A hat offers some protection from excessive sun exposure and it gives some insulation on a cold day. It also forms a base for the head net. Bug jackets now come with built-in head nets. One supplier is Trailhead. Gloves protect the hands while clearing tent sites, making new portage trails or clearing old ones. On cold days gloves keep paddling hands warm. They are also useful for handling hot pots while cooking.

Of particularly high priority to me is having dry wool socks. I want to always have at least one dry pair in my pack. On a wet night I won't put them on until I get into the tent. I insist on wool because of its superior insulation. Pure wool doesn't hold up well with long use so wool reinforced by nylon is best. Some people wear neoprene socks instead of wool, at least while paddling.

Lightweight, long-sleeved shirts are best for when the bugs are out. Other shirts are for colder nights. Polypropylene fabric is very warm, even when wet. An alternative is a heavy wool or insulated jacket. Sweaters are not recommended because when soaked, they loose their shape and become extremely heavy. On one trip my paddling partner had a wool sweater that got wet. He spent the better part of a week trying to get it dry enough to wear. I prefer trousers that are at least partially synthetic. Although they are not as warm as cotton or wool, they dry much faster. Blue jeans dry very slowly. Wet suits are heavy, but much can be said for the warmth they provide. All clothing should be packed in plastic bags.

Plastic rain suits are low-priced, available at any dime store, roll up into tiny lightweight packages and are excellent as long as it doesn't rain. —Bob Cary in *The Big Wilderness Manual*

Cheap plastic rain suits snag and rip on everything during a portage. Worse, they trap body moisture, so with exercise one becomes soaked from the inside. Cloth-reinforced rain pants are satisfactory. An alternative is the cagoule—a three-quarter-length parka that can be pulled over the knees when paddling. However they too shut in body moisture. Gortex is a waterproof fabric that breathes, but it is quite expensive. Despite my personal aversion to rain pants, I realize that they do offer protection for the bowman from waves breaking over the bow.

Falls at the end of the Fond du Lac River, Saskatchewan.

Fishing gear: Long-nose pliers are useful for removing lures from northern pikes, which have vicious teeth. I keep my gloves handy for walleyes. A landing net is bulky and unnecessary. Even a large fish can be landed by firmly gripping it behind the gills. A fishing kit should contain extra swivels, extra leaders, and at least a half dozen lures including spoons (Daredevils) and feathery types (Mepps). Band-aids packed in the fishing kit will obviate opening a separate first aid kit when a hook catches a finger rather than a fish.

Canoe gear

Some gear should be considered as common for the canoe:

Item	No	wt (oz)	wt (g)
17-foot Kevlar® canoe	1	8640.0	24550
sail with bag	1	6.5	180
cover	1	8.5	240
sponge and bailer	1	3.0	90
water filter	1	32.0	910
painters (25 ft)	2	16.0	450
canoe repair kit	1	8.5	240
paddles	3	96.0	3380
short pieces of rope		4.0	110
Total weight: 71 lbs, 7 oz (3.0 kg)			

My Kevlar® canoe, which weighs 55 pounds, is much lighter than most canoes. Aluminum canoes typically weigh 70 to 75 pounds and ABS canoes weigh 75 to 80 pounds. The painters are ¼-inch braided nylon rope with a central longitudinal strand. Braided rope without a central longitudinal fiber is dangerous because it can tangle. The painters are secured to the bow and stern so they can be used for lining the canoe in fast water and securing the craft on shore. Three paddles per canoe are recommended in case one breaks or is lost. The sponge and bailer are kept available for use, but are secured to the canoe with string so they won't float away in case of capsizing. A bailer can be made by cutting the bottom out of an old Clorox bottle or milk jug.

The nature of the canoe repair kit depends on the type of canoe. For aluminum canoes, bolts can replace missing rivets. Black electrician's tape, duct tape, wire, bathtub caulk, small nails, and a universal tool are useful for all canoes. The canoe cover is used in heavy waves to keep excessive water from pouring into the canoe. It is stretched over the gear in the middle and fastened to the gunwales. It can help things stay dry in rain. The use of the sail is covered in Chapter 5. Water filters are necessary in waters infected by *giardia*. This is explained in Chapter 4.

Expedition Gear

Expedition gear includes a cook kit, a first aid kit, food, and a saw as well as a trowel for digging personal latrines. In recent years GPS devices and cell phones have become available for wilderness travel. You can use a GPS to pinpoint your exact coordinates. This isn't usually necessary, but it is helpful in case of emergency rescue because rescuers can be advised of exact locations. In case of emergencies, a cell phone can summon help. I personally dislike having someone with a cell phone on the trip. If the trip is not in remote regions, a cell phone can be used for emergency, but too often it can be used just for gabbing with someone back in civilization. This defeats the idea of getting into the wilderness to get away from the "real world." I also don't believe an axe is necessary. A saw is sufficient for cutting wood and is less dangerous.

Someone on the expedition should pack an emergency medical kit. Wilderness medical care is explained in Appendix 4.

Food

As an army marches on its stomach,
so must a canoe expedition paddle on its.

General comments

The two main questions are what to take and how much. I recommend taking only dried food. There are two reasons for this. One is to save weight. On a long trip, the food pack weighs a lot. Water is always available to rehydrate the food. The other is environmental. Dry food can be packed in plastic bags, which can be burned.[1] If you take cans, they should be put in the fire to burn out residuals and then packed out. Do not litter.

Dry food doesn't mean special and expensive freeze-dried meals sold in camping stores for backpackers. There is nothing wrong with commercially packaged freeze-dried meals. However, one can assemble a meal that tastes better and is much less expensive.

---

1   Some people regard burning plastic bags as environmentally unfriendly. Because plastic bags are made from either polyethylene or polypropylene, the only products of combustion are carbon dioxide and water. However, one should make sure that they are completely burned.

Many dry food items can be purchased in the local supermarket. Rice, spaghetti, flour, sugar, noodles, candy, and nuts all have very low moisture contents. Supermarkets also carry dried soups, drink mixes, puddings, sauces, dried potatoes, raisins, and other dry fruits. Asian grocery stores carry dried mushrooms, fish, and shrimp. Dried meat is the big exception. If available, it is quite expensive.

Anyone can dry meat at home. It can be either air dried or dried in a drier, which can also dry fruits and vegetables. More about driers later. Drying eggs at home isn't safe, but dried eggs can be purchased either from hospital and food services, or from commercial outfits. (I buy mine from *The Baker's Catalogue.*)

How much food?

This question can be answered easily by considering the daily energy (calorie) requirements of active adults. An exercising adult needs about 3,000 calories per day. Table I shows that on a dry basis most food contains about 4 calories per gram. Using this figure it is easy to calculate that one person needs (3,000 cal/day)(4 cal/gm) = 750 grams (dry weight) per day. Converting grams into pounds, and taking into account that most dry foods contain 10% moisture, the 750 grams is equivalent to about 1.83 pounds of food per person per day. For cool weather trips, this number can be rounded upward to at least two pounds per person per day. There are no "super high energy" foods. In planning, include neither cooking oil nor alcohol in the calorie count. Commercial freeze-dried meals tend to be a little skimpy, so it is a good idea to weigh them.

John Malo suggests that teenagers may need 3,700 to 4,600 cal per day.[2] Therefore the weight should be increased to account for teenage appetites.

---

2   John W. Malo, *Wilderness Camping*, Colliers Books, NY, 1971.

Energy Content of Dry Food

Food	cal/g (dry weight)	%(dry weight) protein	fat	carbohydrate
Spaghetti	4.1	14	1	84
Rice	4.1	8	0	91
Corn & wheat	4.1	10-12	1	86-89
Potatoes	3.8	8	1	86
Sugar	3.8	0	0	98
Puddings	3.8	8	1	89
Milk (dry)	3.7	38	1	54
Eggs	6.4	38	50	12
Meat (trimmed of fat)	5.0	65-80	16-31	0
Fruit	3.3-3.5	3-6	1	88-94
Peas & beans	3.8	23-25	2	69-71
Fats & oils	8.6-9.0	0	100	0
Nuts & seeds	5.9-6.4	18-25	48-59	19-31
Chocolate (semi-sweet)	5.1	1	36	58
alcohol	6.9	0	0	100[3]

Summary: The calorie content of all carbohydrates and all proteins is very close to 4 calories/gram. The energy content of fats is about 9 calories/gram.

---

3   The water content of different liquors varies from 25% (150 proof) to 55% (80 proof).

"Dry" foods do contain moisture. The amount varies from 1% for noodles to about 10% for spaghetti and peas.

Moisture Content of Dry Food

Food	% water
spaghetti	10.4
rice	9.6
corn	12.0
wheat flour	12.0
potatoes (dry)	5.2
noodles	1.0
puddings	5.2
chocolate	1.0
margarine	16.0
vegetable oil	0.0
peanuts	1.6
almonds	5.2
sunflower seeds	5.9
beans	10.5
peas	10.5
vegetables (most)	5.0
apricots ("dehydrated")	3.5
apricots ("dried")	25.0
raisins	18.0
apples ("dry")	25.0

I usually pack food for an extra day or two in case the trip takes longer than planned. Any fish that are caught are an extra treat. However, it isn't wise to count on them. Those concerned with nutritional content (vitamins and vital minerals) can carry vitamin supplements.

Lower Stikine River, Alaska.

How to pack food

It is very annoying to try to assemble a meal in the bush from several different bags, especially if one is exhausted at the end of a long day and the black flies are out, or if it is raining or past dusk. Much of this frustration can be avoided by careful packing of food before the trip starts. The scheme is to use a separate plastic bag for each meal. A lunch bag contains all the food necessary for that lunch. Similarly a dinner bag contains the entire dinner, except for soup and dessert. These are packed in separate soup and dessert bags. Having soups in a separate bag allows the party to forego soup on a hot day or have two soups on a cold day. A separate desert bag allows the group to choose the dessert after dinner, because sometimes the fire isn't the proper kind for baking.

Common items like coffee, tea, sugar, salt, pepper margarine, oil, and Brillo pads are put in a separate bag that I call "the kitchen."

Menus:

Breakfast: My breakfasts always contain Tang and coffee. Hot cereal breakfasts (2 packets per person) with brown sugar permit an early start. Dry cereal like granola makes another quick breakfast. On more leisurely mornings, eggs or pancakes may be cooked. Syrup can be made from brown sugar, with or without maple flavoring. Bacon bits go well with eggs or pancakes. I make dehydrated sausage from seasoned, ground, and dried lean pork. It is especially tasty when rehydrated with some added oil.

Lunch: I recommend lunches consisting of six items:

1) Drink mix – ice tea or Kool-Aid
2) Nuts – peanuts, mixed nuts, or sunflower seeds
3) Cookies[4] or crackers – kinds that won't crush easily
4) Dried fruit – either store-bought or home-dried, peaches, apricots, raisins, pears, bananas, etc.
5) Jerky – 1 to 1.5 ounces per person
6) Candy

Lunch is the heaviest meal of the day. You can "squirrel" some of it into your pockets to nibble while paddling.

---

4   Springerle cookies are a favorite. They are anise-flavored cookies made without any shortening. Springerle are very hard and don't break up in the pack. I use the recipe in *Joy of Cooking*.

Dinners: Typical dinners include:

Sunset supper – potatoes, ham, and peas with a cheese sauce. A passable cheese sauce can be made from grated cheddar cheese and powdered milk. Measure out the dry milk at home.

Spaghetti – This consists of spaghetti noodles and sauce. The sauce can be made from a can of tomato sauce (dried at home), dried tomatoes, dried hamburger, onions, and mushrooms. Real garlic and parmesan cheese add variety.

Baked beans – Canned baked beans can be dried. I remove the fat and drain the juice into a pot. The drained beans are dried on a tray and the juice is boiled down and then dried as leather. A liberal amount of dried ham or pork adds taste. This is a quick meal to rehydrate in the bush.

Chili – Basically this is dried navy, pinto, or great northern beans together with dried hamburger and perhaps a little tomato sauce. If the beans are soaked and partially cooked and then dried at home, they will rehydrate much faster in the field. Onions and garlic can be added. Not everyone likes the same amount of chili, so the flavoring can be added personally after cooking.

Beef stroganoff – Stroganoff can be made either from beef jerky or dried hamburger, dried mushrooms, noodles, and dried stroganoff sauce from the supermarket.

Chop suey – This consists of rice with a corn starch-base sauce that contains either dry chicken or dry turkey, dried celery, mushrooms, onions, and even water chestnuts (dried from a can). Dry noodles on top and soy sauce add zest. A variant is pork chop suey.

Shepherd's pie – The basis of Shepherd's pie is hamburger, mashed potatoes, and peas. Other vegetables may be added.

Rice and sausage – The sausage is lean pork boiled, ground, seasoned with sausage seasoning, and then dried. Oil should be added after rehydration to give a sausage-like texture. Peas or another vegetable may be added.

These are just a few suggestions. We have a bit of fun during the winter months dreaming up new recipes. Each member of the crew should prepare at least one dinner; it is an opportunity to be imaginative. I had a paddling colleague who often prepared a special Korean treat with bean curds and noodles.

Having different people cook dinner different days adds variety. In this way, no one person gets stuck with this chore every night. There is a widespread story about a party in which no one wanted to cook. They decided to draw straws to see who would cook first. The first person to complain about the food would automatically become cook. The trouble was that no one complained and the cook seemed to have a permanent job. The cook finally collected moose droppings that he found on the trail and fried them. During dinner, one of the crew finally burst out, "These taste like moose turds! ... but good!"

Drink mixes: A separate bag of drink mixes (lemonade, ice tea, Kool-Aid) allows for an end-of-the-day refreshment.

Soups: Individual soup packets are packed in a separate bag so each person can choose his/her own.

Desserts: These are packed separately. They are mostly puddings and biscuits. The puddings are the instant variety that needs no cooking. Mousse is a nice treat. The required dry milk is packed with each pudding. Occasionally someone may try something more complicated. I once made a pineapple upside-down cake with cake mix, brown sugar, and dried pineapple. A strawberry shortcake was made from dried strawberries and biscuit mix. Popcorn is light and can be cooked over the fire in a pot with a lid.

Salad: A barely passable salad can be made from dehydrated carrot slices, cucumber, and radish slices. It might be welcome after a week with no fresh food.

The kitchen

The kitchen contains cooking oil, coffee, tea, sugar, brown sugar, condiments, a few paper towels, Brillo pads, and perhaps honey, decaf coffee, and fresh garlic. When planning, remember that 1 quart = 2 pints = 4 cups = 32 tablespoons = 96 teaspoons.

One quart of margarine is equivalent to 1 tablespoon per person, per day for 4 people for 8 days.

One pint of instant coffee will make 2 cups (1.5 tsp each) per person, per day for 4 people for 8 days.

One pint of sugar is equivalent to 2 teaspoons per person, per day for 4 people for 8 days. How much oil to carry depends on how many fish will be fried. All meat has been de-fatted so a dollop of oil in each dinner is welcome. One quart for 40 man-days is probably enough.

One Brillo pad should last two days.

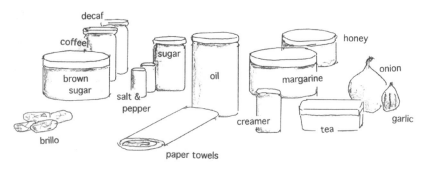

Food to Pack for 4 people for 10 days

sugar	1 lb
brown sugar	2 lbs
coffee, decaf & tea	8 oz
creamer	4 oz
oil	2 lbs
margarine	1 lb
salt & pepper	3 oz
onion & garlic	8 oz
Brillo pads	5 oz
paper towels	6 oz
misc. spices	2 oz
total	**10 lbs**

*Camp at the first canyon on the Mountain River,
Northwest Territories.*

Supplies like coffee, tea, cocoa, honey, and creamer are up to individual tastes. It is easy to underestimate how much brown sugar will be consumed as it is used on cereals and in tea.

Food from the land

Often some food can be gathered from the land. I've tried cattail roots, boiling them several times and discarding the water, only to find them far too bitter to eat. I've also tried what I thought were fiddlehead ferns, but again they were too bitter to eat. Blueberries in the late summer are good. They may be added to pancakes or eaten with breakfast cereal. Occasionally a scallion can be found, but the greatest success has been with morels. Fortunately morels are not easily confused with other mushrooms. They have a honey-comb-like upper portion composed of a network of ridges around valleys. They may be found under deciduous trees, which are usually aspens in the north. Fried with a little garlic, they are quite tasty. After reading about river-bottom clams in *Survival of the Birchbark Canoe* by John McFee, I decided to try them. Sautéed in garlic-flavored margarine, they are at first delicious, but then I soon discovered that I was chewing and chewing and the flavor of the garlic margarine was gone so I was chewing a mouthful of rubber. Sometimes crayfish can be found. These are like tiny lobsters, but it is difficult to find enough for a whole meal.

Cooking and eating utensils

It's best if each person is responsible for his/her own Sierra cup or bowl, fork and spoon. I like to have an extra cup for drinking.

My cook kit consists of three pots (1½ quarts, 3 quarts, and 1½ gallon) with lids, a coffee pot, two plastic cups for measuring, two aluminum plates, and two frying pans with detachable handle, one of which is a lid for the largest pot. The set comes with more cups and plates but these are unnecessary if each person has their own. With the cook kit, I also pack an extra frying pan with folding handle, large fork, large spoon, and mitten. Everything is carried in a cloth bag.

Drying food

Jerky was an important food of the plains Indians and western explorers. The word derives from the Quecha word *charqui* meaning dry meat. It is not related to the English *jerk*, meaning to pull rapidly. The first step in preparing jerky is removing as much fat as possible. It is the fat turning rancid that limits the storage life of jerky. The meat should be cut into thin strips about ⅛-inch thick and put into a marinade. Poultry and pork are best dried after cooking.

A basic recipe for a marinade is 2 quarts of water, ½ cup of vinegar and ⅛ cup of salt. Various seasonings can be added to this. Pepper is almost always used. For beef, I like a lot of garlic powder. Worcestershire sauce, soy sauce, hot sauce, and curry are other possibilities. Poultry seasoning goes well on chicken and turkey. For pork sausage, I use a mixture of spices: 2 parts sage, 2 parts thyme, 2 parts marjoram, 1 part savory, and 1 part coriander in addition to 4 parts pepper and the salt. It's fun to try different variations.

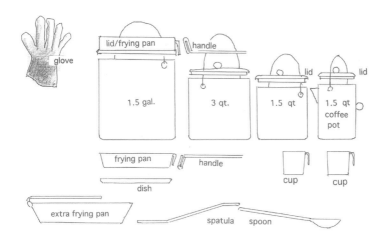

The meat is soaked in the marinade for 6 to 24 hours. It should be turned several times so all of the meat is exposed to the marinade. Dry marinade is also possible. *How To Dry Foods*, by H. P. Brooks, has a number of recipes.

To make hamburger and ground sausage, I start with defatted meat. With hamburger, I cut it into strips, marinade it, and dry it for a couple of hours. I then grind it and continue drying. Grinding dry meat requires a great deal of effort. For sausage, I boil the pork, then season, grind, and dry it. I prepare ground chicken by boiling it first and then grinding it with seasoning.

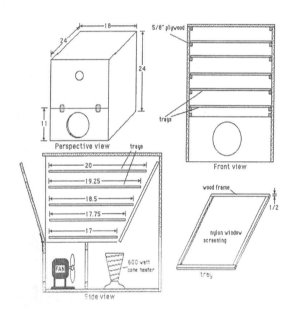

Drying may be done either in air or in a drier.[5] Plans for a simple homemade hot air drier are shown here. This is a slight modification of a drier described by Kirk.[6] The temperature in the drier should be between 140° and 160°F. A simple test for whether the meat is sufficiently dry is to bend it. If it is brittle, it is done.

Vegetables and fruit may also be dried in a hot-air drier. Fruit keeps its color better if blanched in an ascorbic acid (vitamin C) solution. Most vegetables should be sliced or at least have their

---

5   Plans for a drier, *Fruit Drier Plan* 6202, can be obtained from Cooperative Extension, U.S.D.A., Roberts Hall, Cornell University, Ithaca NY 14853.

6   Dale E. Kirk. *How to Build a Portable Electric Food Dehydrator*, Oregon State University, Extension Service Circular 855 – printed by the U.S. Government Printing Office 1977 0-225-030.

skins broken although this isn't necessary with frozen peas. I often dry tomato slices, peas, asparagus, and mushrooms. Dried beans can be soaked, cooked slightly, and then dried. The advantage is that they rehydrate much faster than they normally would. Apples, peaches, pears, and apricots all dry well. Bananas aren't worth drying because dried bananas are so cheap. Leathers can be made of applesauce, juiced fruits, and tomato sauce. If the sauces are too liquid, they may be thickened by boiling off some of the water. The thickened sauce is poured on a piece of Saran on a cookie sheet and dried. It should be removed from the drier while still pliable enough to roll up.

Winter is the best time for drying because the humidity is very low. The shelf lives of dried foods are greatly increased if they are stored in airtight containers in a cool place, even a freezer.

Two canoes at a campsite in the French River Delta, Ontario, at the corner where four rivers join.

Camp on the Drowning River, Ontario.

Campfire baking

It took me several years before I learned how to bake biscuits without burning them. The trick is to bake them under the fire, rather than on top of it. Two frying pans are used. The dough is put into the smaller pan and the bigger one is inverted to form a lid. After a good number of coals have formed, the fire and coals are scraped out of the fire pit. Place the assembled pans into it and then cover

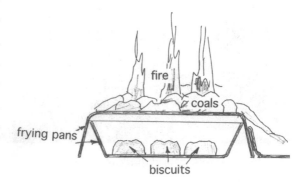

them with coals and fire. I usually use the time on the box, but I have no idea whether I have the prescribed temperature. When the baking time has elapsed, the pans are removed. This procedure destroys a well-set fire, so it is postponed until all of the rest of the cooking is complete. In addition to biscuits, cake and even bread can be baked. If a prepared mix is used, it can be packed in a Ziplock bag with required milk and instructions.

Bannock is the traditional bread of the north woods. There are numerous recipes for bannock, but all rely on baking powder as a rising agent. One recipe calls for 1 part baking powder to 9 parts flour with just enough water to hold it together so it can be formed into small bricks about one inch thick, two inches wide, and four inches long. This is fried in an oiled frying pan.

Grace

On the Bloodvein River, Ontario and Manitoba, our group had lunch with 11 boys and a companion group of 12 girls from St. Cloud, Minnesota. What a great bunch! They taught us their grace:

Les Voyaguers Grace
For food, for raiment, for life, and opportunity,
for sun and rain, for water and portage trails,
for friendship and fellowship,
we thank thee, O Lord.

Making Camp

One's camp is one's home—even for a night.

The hours that we spend in camp leave us with some of the most rewarding memories. Camp time is a time for repairing gear and engaging in such activities as exploring, swimming, fossicking[1], fishing, painting, reading, and taking photographs. An expedition that leaves no time for such activities becomes drudgery. These wilderness treks are recreational and should always include fun.

When and where to make camp

There are a number of considerations in selecting a campsite. An ideal campsite should have:

1) level dry spots for tents
2) a good landing spot where canoes can easily be unloaded
3) easy access to water

---

1   *Fossicking* is an Australian word that means "searching about or rummaging for gold, precious stones or fossils." It seems to be a most appropriate description for beachcombing and fossil hunting.

Camp on the South Nahanni River, Northwest Territories.

4) an adequate supply of firewood
5) a good safe place for a fire
6) shelter in case of a storm, or a good breeze if bugs are a problem
7) comfortable places to sit with a nice view

Of these considerations, suitable spots for tents and ease of landing are most important. Also look for reasonable spots for fishing and swimming. Overhanging tree limbs can be very useful for keeping food packs out of the reach of bears and other hungry critters. A campsite's desirability sometimes hinges on the expectation of bad weather or how bad the bugs are.

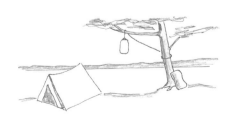

Camp should be made early enough so there is plenty of daylight. (See Appendix 5 for time of sunset.) There should be sufficient time to set up tents, gather wood, make a cooking fire, eat, and clean dishes before dark. One may also need daylight to wash clothes and dry wet ones. Additional time should be allotted for leisure activities. Often, a good bit of time elapses between the decision to make camp and selection of a suitable campsite. How much time depends on the nature of the country and how tired the crew is. Then there is the "campsite game." In the campsite game, one person goes ashore to assess whether a site is suitable while the others await his decision. If he says no or waffles, they paddle on. If the decision is favorable, others may go ashore and put thumbs down on the site. However, now the job of selecting a suitable site shifts to the naysayer. To avoid this responsibility, most crew members remain non-committal. Thus the campsite game is often one of cooperative indecision. No one knows how the game originated. It seems to be instinctual.

Canoer's lament

Why do we never see at five o'clock
The places we see at three?
Oh we never do
We just go howling on until our tummies rumble
And thunder comes boom, boom, boom inside and out
And Ovaltine the crew does shout.
I wish I were at home in bed
The window shut and candle at my head
I'll never roam no more.

As a rule it is wise not to run a rapid or start a long portage after about 5 p.m. Sometimes a very good campsite is at the end of a portage trail, and falls are often nice places to camp. A half portage may be made, with some of the party setting up camp and the others going back for a second carry. If wet gear needs to be dried, start looking for a campsite early. A glance at the map will tell whether there is swampy or high ground ahead.

Chores

Camp chores begin once canoes are unloaded. It makes no sense for everyone to do the same thing. Usually only one person is required to erect a tent. Others may gather firewood, or, if appropriate, dig a fire pit and start the fire. Someone needs to get water for dinner. Sometimes an area needs clearing out. After a few days, the division of labor will become automatic. Wet clothing should be hung up as soon as possible. Wet sleeping bags demand priority. On a long trip it is wise to occasionally do laundry. In some parties, chores are assigned, but I have found that usually people can see what needs to be done without being told.

It is wise to pull canoes well up on shore and secure their painters to something solid. Even though it may be calm at the moment, a strong wind may blow up during the night and shift the canoes. I have vivid memories of seeing one of our canoes windborne on the shores of Wunnummin Lake, Ontario.

Tent pitching

The best location for the tent is dictated by several factors. Because tents are flammable, they should be well away from the fire. Where to pitch a tent and which way it should face depend on the volume of bugs. A breezy place will have fewer bugs. If a storm is threatening, a sheltered place is a better choice. Slope of the ground is very important. I prefer having my head slightly higher than my feet. Hollows should be avoided although bumpy ground may be leveled by flattening the high spots and filling the low ones. Avoid small bushes rather than cutting them down. Cut stumps have a way of pushing into the tent floor. Getting into the tent and rolling around, before the tent is staked may reveal small annoying stones. Once erected, something heavy should be put into the tent to keep it from blowing away. Once on the North French River, Ontario, one of our tents flew away before we could stake it down.

Some people advise against camping on sand because it gets into everything. Yet a beach is often very attractive and if care is taken, the sand problem is manageable. Remember, however, that sand is very hard.

A ground cloth under the tent (a.k.a. a footprint) will help keep dampness out, but it should never extend beyond the tent floor. If it does, it will serve to direct the water that comes off the fly back to the tent. I have suffered this fate. The best solution is to put the ground cloth inside the tent's perimeter.

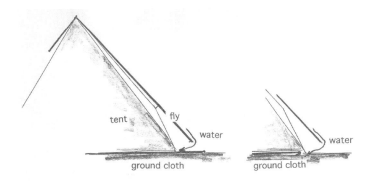

Several factors enter the decision of whether to pitch a tent under trees or in the open. On clear nights there is a much greater temperature drop in the open. The amount of cooling is surprising. Because of radiation to the sky, water in an open pot may freeze even though the air temperature remains above freezing. Ancient Persians made ice by digging deep holes that permitted water to cool as it radiated heat to the sky while being sheltered from warm air.

Packs do not need to be put into the tent, so a tent large enough to accommodate packs is not necessary. Any food in the tent will attract wild animals. There are many stories about hungry or curious bears, but more tents have been ruined by mice that can smell candy or nuts. One's pack can be leaned against a tree and covered with a plastic garbage bag to protect it from rain and dew. All I need inside my tent is a sleeping pad, sleeping bag, enough clothing to make a pillow, a pee bottle, and perhaps a flashlight.

Insects

Mosquitoes and black flies are the bane of the north. They don't like wind or sunshine, so the best place to rest is a windy spot in the sun. Appendix 6 describes insects and repellents in detail.

Fire

In selecting a site for the fire, consideration should be given to ensuring the fire won't spread. If possible, an existing fire pit should be used. Otherwise it is important to dig down past peat to clay or dirt, ripping out any vegetation. Of course this isn't necessary if it is on ledge rock. A ring of stones around the fire will help contain it and serve as handy places to put things. A grate isn't required. Pots or pans for cooking can be placed directly on the fire. Each night before retiring, the fire should be doused completely. No matter how much water is used, it will be dry enough for a breakfast fire. Dry wood for a breakfast fire can be stored under a tarp or canoe.

Large groups that practice no-trace camping may carry a portable steel fireplace. The major disadvantage is the weight: 8 to 10 lbs (3.5 to 4.5 kg). In this case no fire pit or rocks are necessary. The ash remaining after the fire should be packed out after it has completely cooled, or it can be spread across the land.[2]

---

2   For no-trace camping, there are two opinions on how to dispose of ashes from a campfire. In the United States, where the number of canoe campers is high, the Pollution Control Agency and most state park departments recommend spreading ashes around on the land—so they do not pollute the river. On the other hand, Parks Canada recommends that campers in the far north use a fire box and dump the ashes in the river, so no trace is left on land. The flow volume of many rivers in Canada is large enough to dilute any pollution—so it will have little effect on the environment.

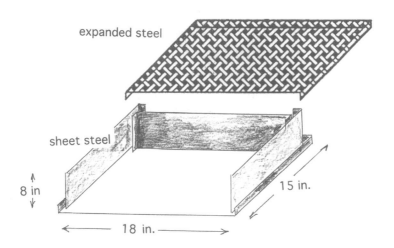

expanded steel

sheet steel

8 in

15 in.

18 in.

Driftwood and dead standing wood are satisfactory for fires. Beaver often chew logs into convenient lengths. The rest can be broken or sawed. Dead birch does not makes good firewood. It is either green or rotten. (The bark keeps the wood from drying out. People who sell birch cordwood prevent it from rotting by splitting it soon after it is cut.) Dead aspen, spruce, and cedar burn well. Although an axe is handy for splitting wood, the chore can be done with a large knife by hitting the back of the blade with another log.

After several days of rain, fires may be hard to start. One way to get reasonably dry kindling is to select standing dry

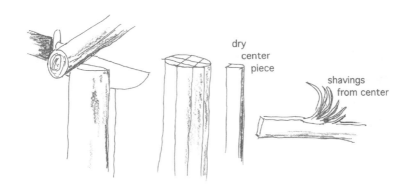

dry
center
piece

shavings
from center

wood at least 2 inches in diameter and split it. The central inch or so is apt to be dry. This can be cut into shavings. Birch bark and candles may also be helpful. Enough wood for breakfast should be gathered before dark and placed under cover, like an overturned canoe. Once the fire is started, a pot of water can be put on so tea, soup, or coffee can be enjoyed while dinner is cooking.

I find my shoes are wet at the end of almost every day. It is tempting to put them by the fire to dry out, but even sneakers won't dry easily and there is always the danger of burning them. It's better to have wet shoes in the morning than burned ones for the entire trip. If the campsite is reasonably dry, I will change into dry socks and a dry pair of sneakers, but only when I am sure that I can keep them dry. In any event, each evening I will put on dry socks just before climbing into my sleeping bag. Wet shoes are put outside the tent under the fly, so as to be ready to put on in the morning. Any temptation to get into dry sneakers in the morning must be resisted, since reluctance to wade in dry shoes can encourage people to do risky things to stay dry.

Water treatment

The three basic groups of contaminants in water are: microorganisms, particulates, and dissolved chemicals. In the wilderness the greatest threat is from *giardia* caused by the *protozoa cyst* common in waters inhabited by beaver. *Giardiasis* is a diarrheal disease caused by a parasite, *giardia intestinalis*, which lives in the intestines. *Giardia* is protected by an outer shell, so it can live outside of the body for a long time. One can become infected either by swallowing anything that has come in contact with the feces of a person or animal that is infected with *giardia*, or by swallowing water contaminated with *giardia*. Symptoms appear in one to two weeks after infection. Doctors can prescribe appropriate drugs. Bacteria such as *e-coli* and *salmonella* may be found near populated areas and in stagnant water. Viruses that infect humans are not common in the wilderness. Chemical contamination is a problem only downstream from industrial areas. Particulates including mud (sand and silt) don't usually affect health but are unsightly and may affect taste. The sizes range from 0.2 to 10 microns for bacteria, 5 to 15 microns for protozoa, and 4 microns for particulates.

Water may be purified by filtration, boiling, or with chemicals. Filters are easy to use and don't affect taste. Water filters cost between $30 and $100. Because the *giardia cysts* are large, they are easily filtered out. The cheaper filters, which have larger pore sizes, are adequate, and they pump more easily and clog less frequently. They remove particulates and the large organisms (including *giardia*) but do not remove viruses or chemicals. One disadvantage is that particulates tend to clog filters. Boiling is effective against all organisms but is slow and leaves a flat taste. In the past halazone (a chloride) was used extensively, but is not effective against all cysts and tastes bad. Iodine is more widely used and is effective against all organisms. However, pregnant women and those with thyroid problems are warned against using iodine.

Rain shelter

A rain shelter can be erected using a polyethylene sheet or other waterproof sheet supported by

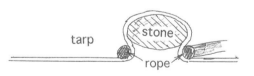

poles or trees. In the absence of grommets, a rope can be attached by wrapping the tarp around a small stone to form a place to tie a line. All polyethylene, torn or not, should be carried out of the bush. Various knots are discussed in Appendix 3.

Drying clothes

As much water as possible should be wrung out of wet clothes before hanging them up to dry. They should be spread out to facilitate drying. Broken twigs will keep socks open. With wool, excess water can be wrung out of the low spots after a while. If you must use the fire for drying, wait until the cooking is done and don't put things too close to the fire.

Latrine and refuse

In days of old when knights were bold
and toilets weren't invented
They left their load beside the road
And walked off so contented.

Latrines should be dug at least 100 yards away from the water. Use a trowel to dig a hole 4 to 6 inches deep and bury your leavings. Some groups burn toilet paper rather than bury it because of concern that small animals will dig it up. If you place some brush over your spot, the next person is less likely to accidentally use it. Care in disposing of human waste is not only important for aesthetics—human waste is one of the major means by which *giardia* is spread. The subject is treated in detail in *How to Shit in the Woods* by Kathleen Meyer (10-Speed Press, 2nd edition, 1994).

After cleaning fish, the offal can be thrown into the lake or river where it will be eaten by other fish or by birds. However, in heavily traveled regions, it is better to bury the offal away from the campsite. If refuse is left on shore, it will attract bears. Paper and plastic trash should be burned. Everything else should be carried out of the wilderness.

Breaking camp

If I roll up my mattress and stuff my sleeping bag upon waking in the morning, my tentmate has more room to prepare his things. As soon as both people are up, the tent can be taken down and stored. An exception can be made if the tent is wet or covered with ice. A spruce bough makes a good broom for sweeping snow off of a tent. If it is raining in the morning, it is tempting to delay taking down tents. Resist that temptation. There is no point in spending a miserable day huddled in a tent. The hours saved by paddling can be better spent leisurely on a sunny day.

Once breakfast is finished, the fire can be doused and everything packed and loaded. One person should be assigned to make a careful inspection of the campsite for things that have been overlooked.

Waiting for the wind to abate on Wabakimi Lake, Ontario.

Lake Paddling

General paddling

Normally the bow and stern persons should paddle on opposite sides of the canoe. This allows the turning effect of the bow and stern strokes to partially cancel each other. The cancellation is not complete, however, because the stern paddler's stroke has the larger turning effect. An experienced paddler can paddle on one side for hours, but occasionally changing sides relieves monotony when paddling long stretches. Changing position can relieve cramps. I have a friend who occasionally sits on the stern plate for a change.

On flat water, all steering should be done from the stern. If the bow person wants to change direction, this should be communicated to the stern paddler. This rule does not always hold in rapids, but in lakes it makes no sense for the bow person to try to steer.

A canoe should be loaded so that it is nearly level. If this is not possible, the bow should be higher than the stern. For this reason the heavier person usually takes the stern position. A solo paddler should sit in the middle just behind the center unless there is no wind, in which case paddling from the bow seat sitting backward may be more comfortable. Paddling alone in the stern raises the bow so much that the canoe won't track and makes the canoe harder to control in the wind.

Paddles should be chosen for comfort. The length should be such that one hand can comfortably grip the shaft just above the blade (at the balance point) and hold it just above water level while the other hand is almost horizontal with the shoulders. Because the bow seat is usually lower than the stern seat, the bow paddle should be shorter.

Paddling strokes

Most of the work paddling should be done by twisting the torso rather than by bending the arms. Pushing the paddle by bending the elbows is tiring if done for a long stretch of time. It is possible to keep both arms almost straight throughout the paddling stroke. Although this is a bit awkward, it is a useful exercise because it forces one to apply the impetus by twisting the waist. A bit of practice with straight arms demonstrates how little the arms need to be bent.

While the paddle is being returned forward after completion of the stroke, it should be *feathered.* Feathering is twisting the paddle so the blade is parallel to the water and the direction of motion. There are two reasons for feathering. One is that it decreases the wind resistance, which is important in a headwind. The more important reason is that if the paddle is feathered, it needn't be lifted very high on the return stroke. Although this saves only an inch or two, the total effort saved over an entire day is appreciable.

The J-stroke is the most basic stroke for the stern person. Paddling on one side tends to turn the canoe in the opposite direction. This can be corrected if the stern person twists the paddle at the end of the stroke so the power face of the blade is facing outward and pushes outward as the paddle passes the hip so as to form a "J." The bow paddler should never execute a J-stroke.

Speed

A speed of 2.5 to 3 mph can be maintained with steady paddling and no headwind. Anything much faster requires excessive effort, because the water resistance rises rapidly with speed (see Appendix 8). In open water one may estimate the canoe speed by noting how long it takes a floating leaf, bug, or piece of scum to pass two points of the canoe. The speed in ft/second estimated this way can be converted to mph by multiplying by 0.68 (approximately 2/3).

Headwinds

When there are heavy headwinds, hugging the shoreline gives some lee but only a little, because winds tend to be channeled by the shore. On the other hand, whatever lee afforded is well worth the slight extra distance that has to be paddled. The occasional shelter provided by a point of land is very welcome. Just being able to stop and rest for a moment without being blown backward is a relief. There are other advantages of following the shore. On a lake waves are not as high as in the middle and it is safer in case of a mishap. Furthermore, being near the shore allows one to watch birds and small animals.

The extra distance that must be paddled by following the shore is less than most people think. A simple mathematical analysis shows that the percent extra distance resulting from deviating by an angle, θ, from a straight line course equals 100/(1-cos θ). A 15° deviation adds only 3.5% to the distance and even a 30° deviation adds only an extra 15.5%.

*A route along the shore that deviates 15°
from a direct line is only 3.5% longer.*

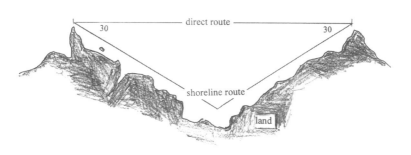

*A route along the shore that deviates 30°
from a direct line is only 15% longer.*

It seems psychologically impossible to paddle against a wind with anything but full effort. There is good reason for this. Light paddling results in only slightly diminished speed in calm weather, but may not keep the canoe from going backward in a strong headwind. I find myself counting paddle

Shake's Lake in Alaska off the Stikine River.

strokes whenever I paddle into the wind. If our course is along a shore, I try to estimate the number of strokes to a certain rock or a tree. This mental exercise staves off boredom.

Lee

Whenever I paddle into a strong headwind I long for the little bit of lee that is offered by the shore ahead. When winds blow off a cliff or a dense growth of trees, a back eddy may be near the shore. At some point from shore, the wind divides and there its velocity is zero. Relative calm is nearer the shore. With an abrupt cliff, the stagnation point is at a distance from the cliff about seven times the height of the cliff.[1] Of course the wind pattern will be somewhat different if the cliff is not vertical.

---

1   A. S. Neto, D. Grand, O. Métais and M. Lesieur, *Journal of Fluid Mechanics*, v. 256, 1993, pp. 1-25.

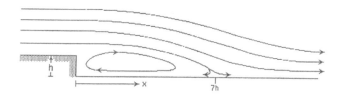

A simple way of estimating the ratio of the distance to a cliff to its height is by extending one's arm with a clenched fist. When the cliff appears as large as the fist, it is about seven times as far away as its height. This is the point at which the first lee effect can be expected. This method is exact if your fist measures 4 inches and your arm length is 28 inches.

Sailing

After paddling into a headwind, a tailwind is most welcome because it offers a chance to sail. I recommend a method of sailing that evolved over many years. Originally, if a favorable wind arose, our party would pull to shore, cut poles and then lash a poncho to them. Because this took so much time, we sailed infrequently. Now we carry lightweight nylon sails with long pockets open at the bottom and closed at the top. Paddle handles can be slipped into the sleeves to form two hand-held masts. Such sails are very light and take up little space. They have taken me many miles, relieving the monotony of lake paddling.

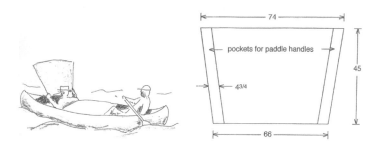

Hand-held sail (left) and a sail plan (right)
dimensions in inches.

Two canoes can be sailed together as a catamaran. This affords a chance for socializing, planning strategy, and eating lunch while underway. At first we lashed the two together with poles. However, this nearly caused a catastrophe on Wunnummin Lake, Ontario. The tailwind became so strong that water began to well up in the six inches between the two canoes. After this episode, we decided to hold the canoes together with two paddles, with the ends held by the legs. One stern-man can steer while the other distributes lunch. Disassembly in an emergency is almost instantaneous.

Wind velocity

The velocity of the wind increases with height above the water. The higher the sail is held, the greater the force is. The hand-held sail tends to push the bow downward.

Often the wind dies down toward evening, so if the daytime wind is too strong for paddling, one may paddle at night.

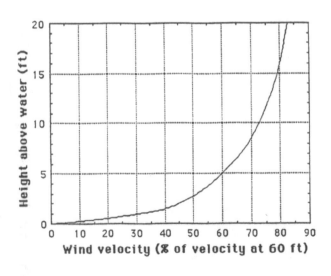

Variation of wind velocity with height.

Finding the direction of flow

Sometimes the area near the outlet of a lake is so filled with reeds that it is difficult to follow the channel that leads to the outlet. Although wind on the water's surface may obscure the flow direction of the water, the direction of flow can be determined by observing the weeds on the bottom. They will point in the direction that the water is flowing.

Loading and unloading

A canoe should be unloaded only when it is fully floating or fully beached. Otherwise it is too tippy.

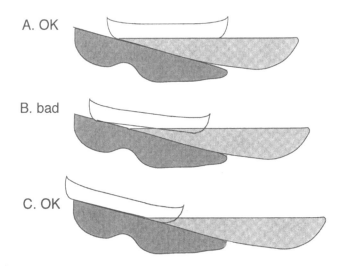

A. OK

B. bad

C. OK

A) The stern person should disembark while the canoe is still floating.

B) If it is pulled partly onto shore it is supported only at the bow and stern and is very tippy.

C) The canoe should be fully beached before unloading.

Portaging

Better safe than sorry.

Whether to portage

Falls must be portaged. No one should ever come upon a falls or rapids by surprise. Usually they can be heard well upstream and are usually, but not always, marked on maps. At a rapids, it is not always obvious whether a portage is required. Sometimes, a quick view from the canoe will make it clear whether the rapid can be run safely. Don't hesitate to stand up to get a good view. However, it is often necessary to give a closer inspection by walking along the shore. A good rule of thumb is to never run a rapids unless you can clearly see a calm spot at the bottom. Water that appears to be run-able can lead to serious difficulties around a bend unless a stopping point is available. On a warm sunny day, it is fun to run a short tricky stretch after first having carried gear to the bottom, because one can dry quickly.

Careful inspection from shore can lead to several possible alternatives: running to the next calm spot, portaging, or lining. Do not be misled by the presence or absence of a portage trail. The need to portage can vary with water level. Sometimes portage trails are mainly used for upstream travel and are not needed for downstream travel. The apparent absence of a portage trail may be because the trail is on the other side of the river or that it is overgrown, or it may start further upstream or further downstream.

Finding the trail

> *That can't be the trail—it looks too good.*
> —Warren Wagner, May 1990

On less-traveled rivers, portage trails may be hard to find because of undergrowth. They are often marked only by twig blazes instead of the infamous axe blazes. Twig blazes are simply broken twigs on a branch. Nothing in nature does this, so twig blazes indicate that someone has walked there. Twig blazes are common because they are so easy to make as one walks along. Double axe blazes are sometimes used to indicate that a tail is making a sharp bend.

Twig blaze.

Double blaze indicating a turn in the trail.

Portage trails seldom follow the most direct route between two bodies of water. They are often on high ground, well away from the water to avoid heavy underbrush and swampy areas. When looking for a portage trail,

"I think we've finally found the portage trail."

check both sides of the stream. What appear to be axe blazes along the river's edge may be marks caused by floating logs during spring runoff at very high water levels. Animal trails are often mistaken for portage trails. Even true tree blazes made by confused humans can be misleading. I recall following a set of blazes that circled back on itself. If many trees have fallen since the trail was last used, it is often necessary to make substantial detours, after which it may be difficult to relocate the trail.

Sometimes portage trails through the woods need be used only in the spring when water levels are high. At lower water levels, ledges along the river may make easier walking than the trail. Often portage trails around falls start dangerously close to the lip of the fall.

If all else fails, one shouldn't be afraid of blazing one's own trail. Because of the difficulty in locating and following trails, it is wise to make the first carry with light packs, leaving the canoe and heavy ones for a second carry. If a trail is new or hard to follow, it pays to back-blaze it. It is easy to become lost while trying to blaze a new trail. It pays to be constantly aware of the surroundings; the slope of the land, noise of the river, direction of the sun, compass bearings, and how these correlate with the map. Getting accustomed to the scale of a map takes a while. Continual reference to the map helps, even if it seems unnecessary. It is much easier to prevent becoming lost than to regain one's bearings when lost.

The portage

A canoe can be carried more easily by a single person than by two people. If two people try to carry a canoe together, they are likely to have trouble keeping in step on rough trails. To get around trees they must thrash through the brush on opposite sides of the trail. If the lead person regards the canoe as flexible, the one in the rear will often have to leave the trail. Although a canoe is relatively heavy, once you have it on your shoulders and balanced, it becomes a bearable load.

There are two viable schemes for deciding how much and what to carry on each leg of a portage. A single carry is attractive if possible. This means that one person carries the canoe and a pack while the other person carries a pack and all of the food and loose paraphernalia (PFDs, maps, etc.). The single carry minimizes walking but requires very heavy loads. Without well-marked portage trails, it is extremely difficult.

In my opinion, the most comfortable portages include two carries. This requires walking the trail three times (two carries over and a return walk), but it is easier on the back than trying to carry everything in one trip. Both people carry a pack over the first time. On the second trip, one person carries the canoe and the other carries a third pack containing shared gear such as food, the saw, cook kit, and tent. Loose gear should be minimized. More packs require more carries.

There are several ways to rig a canoe for carrying. One involves using two paddles wedged or tied between the center thwart and the bow seat. Wedging works well in a Grumman

Too much stuff.

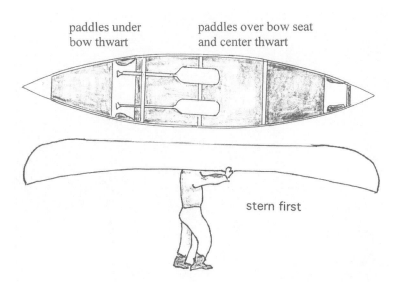

paddles under bow thwart

paddles over bow seat and center thwart

stern first

aluminum canoe. The blades form a yoke. It may be necessary to tie the blades to the center thwart so they don't slip sideward. Even the paddle blades may seem hard after a while so the carry is more comfortable with a life preserver that has shoulder pads. The advantage of this system is that it requires no extra gear and two paddles are transported as well.

Some canoes have a center thwart that doubles as a yoke. If the yoke isn't padded, use something to protect your shoulders. Pads permanently attached to the thwart will become damaged. An alternative is to use pads that can be attached to the center thwart for the carry and then detached.

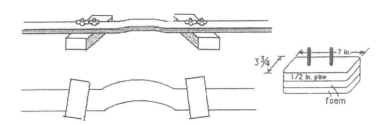

There is a trick to getting a canoe onto your shoulders. Stand beside the canoe, put one hand on each gunwale and then with one quick continuous motion, lift it onto your shoulders. This maneuver is impressive to watch, but I myself don't have enough strength for it. Instead, I stand at one end of the overturned canoe and lift that end while the other end is on the ground. Then I slowly work my way forward to the middle where the canoe will balance on my shoulders. This technique requires only half as much strength as lifting the canoe in a single thrust. Also, you can always ask your partner for help with the initial lift.

*Running a short stretch of fast water in the
Quetico Provincial Park, Ontario.*

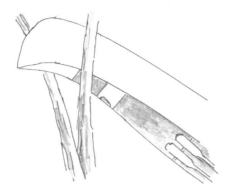

Because getting the canoe onto your shoulders requires so much effort, there is a great reluctance to set it down for a rest during a long carry. When I start to tire, I look for a tree with a fork where I can rest the canoe while I take a break. Lacking a forked tree, two closely spaced ones will do.

Whenever the load seems unbearable, I think about the voyageurs, who each carried up to four pieces (bundles of fur) each weighing 90 pounds on the run. When that thought makes me feel too inferior, I rationalize that it was their profession and I am on holiday. One way of relieving the monotony on a long carry is to stop halfway through, put down the load, and return for a second carry before finishing the first. The second load can be carried all the way across or put down somewhere further on the trail. Breaking up a long carry into several shorter sections provides more periods of relief on return trips. Spotting the next body of water at the end of a long portage brings a great sense of relief.

If a pack is set down halfway across a portage, it is sometimes difficult to find again. This is particularly true in the open areas in the tundra. Yellow packs and yellow life jackets are much easier to spot than any other color. Yellow can be spotted in the distance much easier than red. At far distances and in twilight, red tends to look black.

Memories of miserable portages

I've made several miserable portages. The wind can sometimes lift and twist a canoe while it is being carried in an open area. On the way down a steep bank on the Rupert River in Quebec, a sudden updraft nearly lifted me off the ground. Mucky wet spots are often in the middle of portage trails. On the Pukaskwa, Ontario, I got one foot stuck in the muck and when I pulled it out, my sneaker came off. I have also tripped over a forked stick in the middle of a trail on the Rupert.

On the Horton River, Northwest Territories, we decided that we must portage a single rapid. The rapid itself was quite short, but the only way around it was to climb onto the plateau above it. Then there was no way down, because of a steep cliff. We had to walk three miles (five kilometers) before we could find a passable but very steep slope down to the river.

The end of the Burnside (in Nunavut) has a very long portage. The walking is easy after an initial climb up a hill, but the distance is about four miles. It ends at a sand beach, a short paddle from Bathurst Inlet settlement in Nunavut.

On the Rupert, our party had been warned about a rapids at a sharp corner in the river. The only way to avoid it was to carry across the corner before the rapids. The area had been burned over a few years before and we had to climb under, through, or over a tangle of fallen trees. The carry wasn't more than a tenth of a mile but it was exhausting getting through the mess. Once at the bottom, we looked upstream and the rapids didn't look bad at all. That was one portage we should never have made.

Lining

There may be troublesome stretches of water that seem too dangerous to run but not bad enough to portage. The solution may be lining. Lining involves guiding the canoe as it floats downstream

Rapids on the Bloodvein River, Ontario and Manitoba.

with two painters (ropes), one tied to the bow and the other to the stern. Painters that are about 25 feet (8 m) long allow the canoe to float into the current, but are not so long as to be unwieldy. Before lining, paddles should be tucked into the canoe so there is no chance of snagging the lines on them. Each person handles a painter. Often it is necessary to scramble along the shore and sometimes wade.

If all is going well, the lines should be slack so the canoe can follow its own course. Pulling on the stern line has two effects. It slows the canoe and also brings the stern toward shore. If the stern line is slack and the bowline is pulled slightly, the canoe will turn so that the bow is inclined toward the shore. In this case the current tends to push the canoe further into the current. Thus by controlling the relative tensions on the two lines, the canoe can be steered to some extent. Care should be taken to avoid allowing the canoe to be at too great an angle to the current.

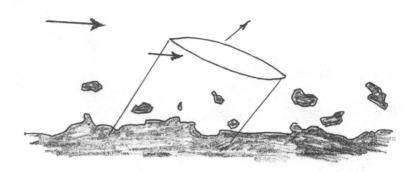

Communication is absolutely necessary while lining. Once, the person with the stern line wanted the stern to drift around an obstacle and shouted "I'm going to let go." The person with the bowline heard only the "let go." The result was a canoe that floated downstream into a pool and had to be retrieved by swimming in cold water.

Trying to exercise too much control by pulling lines is counterproductive as it brings the canoe close to shore where there are more obstacles. When the canoe grounds, it must be pushed back into the current. As a team gains experience, they tend to let the canoe pick its own course.

Pull-overs

Occasionally there is a very short stretch that you won't be able to canoe through or even guide your canoe down from shore. Perhaps near a small fall. In such cases, a pull-over is an alternative to unloading the canoe, transporting it and the gear around and reloading. A loaded canoe can be slid over logs or carried by four people.

Sometimes canoes can be dragged over logs laid across the path. On a trip down the Thelon to Baker Lake, Nunavut, our group met

*Running a stretch of fast water on
the North French River, Ontario.*

heavy headwinds on Beverly Lake, and decided to hug the
north shore. When we came to an island it was decided to take
the northern channel to keep out of the wind. Near the end of
the island the water became too shallow to paddle. Rather
than paddle a mile back or drag the canoes through 200 yards
of very shallow water, it was decided to drag them 100 yards
across sand to the open lake. Fortunately the canoes were
already loaded with logs for firewood. These logs were laid
down to form a "railroad" over which the canoes could be
dragged without unloading. Our strong man provided the
power while the rest of us picked up logs after the canoe had
been over them and laid them in front.

"Ya know, this'd be a nice place to put a river."

When there just isn't enough water to paddle, it may become necessary to get out and drag the canoe over shallow spots.

Swamped canoe on the North French River, Ontario.

River Paddling

The most dangerous animal in the north is dry feet. —R. Kadlec

Paddling strokes

The J-stroke was described in Chapter 5. Other strokes are needed in rapids for quick turning. The bow person is in a position to be most effective in quick maneuvers. The two important strokes are the *draw* and *cross draw*. The draw involves reaching out sideward on the paddling side with the paddle blade parallel to the canoe and pulling it toward the canoe. The effect is to turn the bow toward the paddle side. The cross draw is similar, except it is made on the opposite side without changing hands. By not changing hands the cross draw can be made more quickly and the paddle returned to the original side without changing hands again.

The bow paddler should also know *low brace* and *high brace*. These are for stability, not turning. The low brace involves holding the paddle nearly parallel to the water and leaning on it. This keeps the canoe from tilting toward that side. In the high brace the paddle is held nearly vertically with the blade parallel to the canoe. This too is for stability, keeping the canoe from veering to one

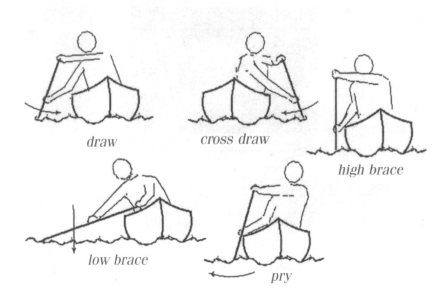

draw   cross draw

high brace

low brace

pry

direction or the other. It is useful where the water currents are confused, as in whirlpool.

The bow paddler can also execute the bow rudder by reaching forward across the bow and placing the paddle blade in the water across the bow. This causes the canoe to turn sharply. However, the violence of the turn may upset the canoe or cause the bowman to lose his paddle, so this maneuver should be used only in extreme emergencies.

bow rudder

The stern paddler can also use draws and braces. On occasion a *pry* may be more effective. The pry is made with the blade initially vertical. The handle is pulled toward the canoe so the blade pivots on the gunwale causing the stern to move away from the paddle side. Any sideways motion of the stern causes the bow to move in the opposite direction.

In a rapids with really large waves, the canoe will tend to plunge from one wave to the next, causing water to break over the bow. A partial remedy for this is for both the bow and stern paddlers to do a strong back paddle as the bow approaches a large wave. This tends to slow the canoe and lift the bow a bit. I found this useful on the Coppermine River, Nunavut.

The ferry is used to cross the river without being swept too far downstream. The canoe is pointed upstream at an angle to the current. The angle to the current will affect how rapidly the crossing is made. The back ferry is similar except that the canoe is angled downstream and the paddlers paddle backward. Here the objective may be to slow the rate of drift through fast water or to be kept from being swept into heavy water on the outside of a bend.

Fishing on the Coppermine River, Nunavut.

Strategy

A long distance should be left between canoes when running rapids. If one canoe gets stuck on a rock, what started as a simple problem is magnified if the next canoe can't stop in time to prevent a collision. If the rapid isn't too long, a good strategy is to let each canoe finish before the next starts. Each canoe can signal the next about potential problems. Everyone should agree on signals used for this purpose. Signals adopted by the ACA (American Canoe Association) are sketched below.

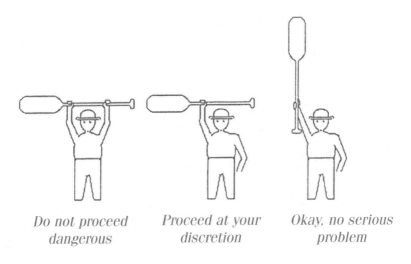

Do not proceed   Proceed at your   Okay, no serious
dangerous   discretion   problem

Rapids

Many rapids can be scouted without going ashore. What you were taught as a child at summer camp about never standing in a canoe should be disregarded. Short of going ashore, standing gives the best view of what lies ahead. It helps one make an initial decision about the best course. Initial decisions, however, should be subject to continual modification. Running a long rapids is like playing chess. Think two or three moves ahead, but be willing to change strategy at any moment.

Once a decision has been made to run a rapids that cannot be scouted effectively from the water, both partners should walk along the shore and decide on their strategy. Packs should be secured to the canoe and the cover, if used, should be snapped in place; all loose items like hats, maps, and loose clothing tucked away. Painters should be handy in case of a mishap. Useful knots are described in Appendix 3.

Unless the canoe is already well upstream of the rapid, it is well to paddle upstream a bit so the rapid can be entered at the best place. Then, approaching the rapid, the stern person can stand for a last assessment of the situation. From upstream a rapid never looks as it did from shore. Kneeling, rather than sitting, as the canoe enters the fast water offers more stability than sitting and also allows one to get one's head high enough to see what is coming. One can put more power into the stroke in a kneeling position than when sitting, although some people find kneeling hard on their legs.

Flow at river bends

Almost always, the current on the outside of a bend has a greater velocity than on the inside. At low water levels, the best chance of avoiding grounding is to paddle the outside. However, this is not always true; sometimes there is a channel on the inside. A useful maxim is *follow the water.* The flow of water usually indicates the path with deepest water. If the water level is high and large waves are the greater danger, an inside course may be advisable. When running the outside of a bend, care should be taken to prevent the canoe from being swept into overhanging limbs or other obstacles. If a limb cannot be avoided, it is better to lean forward than backward. Forward ducking exposes only the back of the head rather than the face.

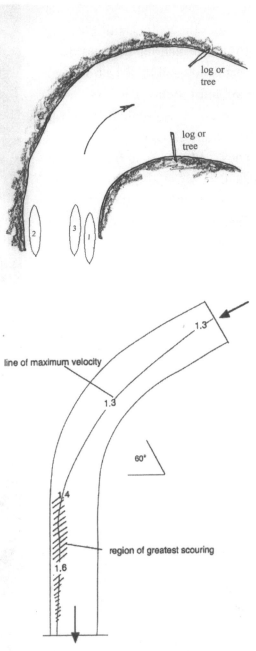

Results from tests on streambeds of trapezoidal cross section. Numbers indicate the water velocity relative to the average velocity.

It is not wise to hug the inside of a bend too closely because it is difficult to see all of the obstacles (1). On the other hand if one swings too wide, the current can sweep the canoe into water with large waves (2). A compromise is near the inside with the canoe pointing slightly to the middle, which gives a better view than hugging the inside and allows one to avoid obstacles (3).

The speed of water in a bend in a river varies with position. At the entrance to the bend the speed is faster at the inside. However, the velocity on the inside decreases into the bend while that on the outside increases so the fastest water is on the outside. This is because the centrifugal force on the water tends to push the water to the outside.

The centrifugal force raises the water level on the outside, making it slightly higher than the inside. As a result, the pressure at the bottom of the outside is a bit greater than the pressure at the bottom of the inside. This sets up a lateral flow with water on the bottom moving from outside to inside and water on the surface moving from inside to outside.

The combination of the lateral and downstream flows results in a helical motion of the water. The high water speed on the outside of the bend causes a high shear stress at the bottom, which results in erosion so the steam becomes deepest on the outside and the banks become much steeper. This erosion on the outside causes a bend to migrate downstream over the years.

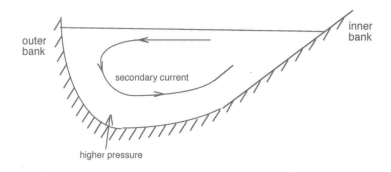

Communication

Clear communication between bow and stern is critical in a rapids. With a novice in the bow, the stern paddler should try to continuously indicate the desired course. If at all possible, the likelihood of a draw should be indicated well in advance of when it will be needed. It is surprising the number of people who will confuse their left and right in the excitement of a rapids. A possible remedy is to agree to the meaning of signals ahead of time. "Draw!" might be used only for drawing on the side being paddled and "cross draw!" or "draw other side!" indicating a draw on the side opposite. The word "right" should

Misty morning on the South Nahanni River, Northwest Territories.

be reserved to indicate direction. It should never be uttered to mean "correct," "yes," or "okay," which would lead to confusion.

Experience in rapids helps one recognize the difference between the white water associated with rocks and the white water of a series of standing waves. The first is to be avoided while the latter indicates deep fast water. An experienced bow paddler will know without advice from the stern when a draw is required and take action to avoid a rock or to keep the bow headed downstream

It is important to keep the bow nearly aligned with the current. If the current is strong, crossing the stream may not be possible. A current of 5 mph is 5.5 ft/s. Only four seconds are available to avoid a rock 30 feet downstream. Therefore, the bow person must take over local tactics, making immediate decisions, and drawing the bow one way or the other around obstacles. There is no time for oral communication.

Often things don't go as planned. If a canoe gets hung up on a rock, get out immediately—otherwise the stern is likely to swing around so that the canoe is broadside to the current. What was at first a minor grounding can quickly turn into a disaster. That is why dry feet are so dangerous. A person with dry feet is likely to be reluctant to jump into the water. Before running a rapid, I sometimes intentionally wet my feet.

If the canoe gets stuck on a rock in such a way that there is no danger of it swinging around, experienced paddlers will take advantage of the moment to reevaluate what lies downstream, instead of instinctively freeing the canoe right away.

At the end of a rapid, where fast water enters slower water, standing waves are likely. Between these waves and the calmer water on either side, there are gradients of water speed. These gradients can be more dangerous than they seem. As a canoe steers out of the fast water, the bow enters the slow water first while the stern is still in fast water, causing the canoe to turn rapidly. Many canoes have flipped at this point. One should leave fast water gradually. A bow draw can keep the bow from exiting too fast and a high brace will help stabilize the canoe and prevent it from turning too fast. Both paddlers should lean downstream.

When approaching a very large wave, a strong back paddle will decrease the tendency for the bow to plunge into the wave. It lifts the bow as well as slowing the canoe.

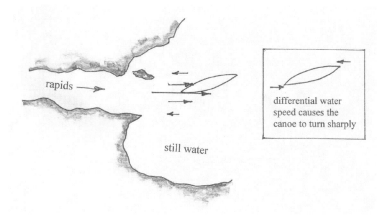

rapids →

still water

differential water speed causes the canoe to turn sharply

Braided Rivers

Some rivers have sections which divide into many channels that rejoin or further subdivide, resembling a complex braid. It is very easy to find yourself running out of paddling water in one of the

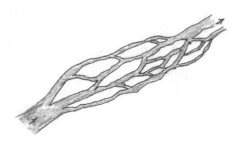

channels of a braided section of river. When a channel divides, one must guess which branch will feed into more flow and which will divide again and again until it is too shallow. Successful navigation requires a lot of luck as well as careful scouting by standing in the canoe. It is quite frustrating to see an adjacent channel several feet lower with plenty of water but no way to get into it. When the canoe ends up grounded the only solution is to get out and drag it over the gravelly bottom. Two suggestions—follow the water and if there are two parallel channels try to get into the lower channel.

Launching and Landing

When pushing out from shore, it is usually easier to let the current swing the stern downstream and turn through 270° than to turn 90° in the opposite direction by forcing the stern upstream. A 270° pirouette maneuver is also useful in a rapid when the canoe has been inadvertently turned to face shore.

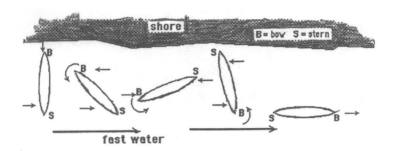

When launching the canoe into fast water, the canoe is perpendicular to the current and the water is moving faster than the canoe so it will tend to force the bottom of the canoe downstream causing the canoe to tip upstream. Leaning downstream while launching will counteract the tipping action. The situation is opposite while landing. As the canoe leaves the fast water, the water is moving more slowly than the canoe and tends to force the bottom upstream, tipping the canoe downstream. In this case, leaning upstream will counteract the downstream tilt.

The sidewise force on the canoe increases with the square of the difference between the velocities of the water and the canoe. A rough estimate of the lateral force on the bottom of the canoe is $F = 40 \ (\Delta V)^2$, where the velocity difference in mph and the force is in pounds. To counteract this, two paddlers weighing 175 pounds each would have to lean a distance, in inches, of about $0.9 \ (\Delta V)^2$. If $\Delta V = 1$ mph, the leaning distance is only 3 inches but if $\Delta V = 3$ mph, the required leaning distance is 8 inches.

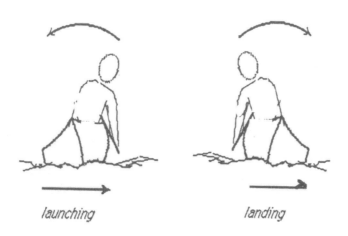

launching   *landing*

Upsets

If there is an upset, it is important to get upstream of the canoe. A canoe full of water weighs several tons and anyone downstream of it is in danger of being crushed between the canoe and a rock. In a rapid, the safest position is on one's back with feet facing downstream. In really cold water, one should try to get out before the body numbs. It is more important to rescue oneself than the canoe. Survival times in cold water vary with the individual, clothing, and water temperature. Typical times are given in Table I.

Table I – Survival times

Water temperature (°F)	Time body remains functional
<40	<10 min
40-50	15-20
50-60	15-40
>60	1 hr +

If the weather is cold, the most useful things to do are to pull the canoe ashore and start a fire. One can die of hypothermia after rescue. Symptoms are blurred speech, clumsiness, and loss of judgment. The wet person should be put near a fire or in a sleeping bag with another person. After getting supplies to shore, everything should be unpacked quickly to keep the dry things from getting wet.

Logs

Logs are nasty obstacles. They are more dangerous than rocks because water flows under them rather than around them. The water flowing around a rock helps direct the canoe around it. When a canoe swings broadside to a log, there is the risk of a capsize because the water acting on the bottom tends to tip the canoe upstream. Getting out of the canoe onto a log is trickier than getting onto a rock. The

Strong winds on Schulz Lake on the Thelon River, Nunavut.

best advice is to avoid logs unless it is possible to run the bow up onto the log so the canoe can be pulled over. If the log isn't too high, this can be done by ramming the log head-on while both persons lean back. If the canoe is run about one-third of the way onto the log, both persons can jump out and haul it over. However if the canoe is run less than one-third of the way onto the log, it is likely to capsize.

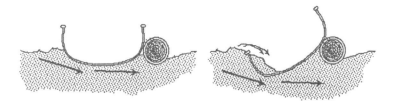

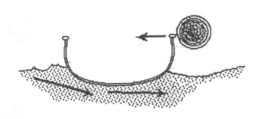

One of my first canoe trips in Canada was on the Abinidong River. We were all neophytes. Early the first morning, we came unexpectedly on a logjam. The first canoe pulled up broadside to it and was promptly sucked under. The second canoe did the same thing and suffered the same fate. Fortunately everyone got out safely and the remaining three canoes stopped upstream. Hours were spent sawing and extracting logs, cutting poles for prying and attaching ropes to the canoes. The first canoe was finally extracted by prying with poles and tugging on ropes attached to the canoe. After more logs were removed and with repeated prying and tugging, we freed the second canoe an hour later. We quickly portaged around the logjam and made camp. With clothes and gear hung on every available tree, our campsite looked like a Brooklyn tenement.

High logs can create an even greater danger of tipping than low logs because there is a greater turning action with the log pushing upstream on the gunwale while the water pushes downstream. If the log is high enough, the canoe may have room to pass under while the paddlers climb over.

On the White River, Ontario, I stopped to scout a minor rapid. After another canoe ran through the rapid, my partner and I decided to run it. We got into our canoe, which was facing upstream, just above a tree that had fallen into the river. I knew that we needed to paddle upstream to get around the tree. However as we pushed off, the bow got into the current and rapidly swung the canoe broadside to the current so that we drifted into the tree. My partner in the bow was able to climb out onto the tree, but I was swept under it as the canoe capsized. I was able to get one hand onto the tree trunk as I slid under the water, but I wasn't strong enough to pull my head above water level. The current was so strong that I finally lost my grip on the trunk. I was sure that all was over for me. Suddenly, I found myself floating downstream on my back, feet first and knew that I had somehow miraculously survived. The lesson I learned was to beware of launching just upstream of an obstacle.

Poling

In shallow water a canoe can be propelled by poling rather than by paddling. The poler stands in the canoe. For poling on the right side, the left foot is a bit forward of the right and the pole is pushed into the bottom just aft of the right foot. The usual technique is a hand-over-hand climb up the pole. After the thrust, the pole is lifted from the water and flipped forward.

Poling can be done along the shore of a lake or for upstream travel in a river. Some claim that it can be used to make headway upstream against a strong current, though I have never used the technique. Poling can be done either solo or in tandem, the latter requiring well-timed coordination. The pole should be 10 to 14 feet long and about an inch in diameter. Sometimes a steel shoe is fitted to the bottom of the pole, but this is not necessary.

Fishing and Leisure

A canoe trip should be enjoyable. Different people like different activities. Some like to fish. Others prefer photography, hiking, scenery gazing, swimming or just resting with a good book to read. Some people play cards in the evening. I like painting watercolors. Leisure activities require some forethought during packing. One must pack the necessary fishing gear, photographic equipment, hiking boots, reading material, cards, or painting supplies.

Fishing

I am no expert fisherman, but I have learned from watching others:

1. You don't need a net to land fish. Even a five-pound (2 kg) fish can be landed by firmly grasping it behind the gills.
2. The best lures for walleyes and northern pike seem to be either spoons (e.g. daredevils) or feathery things (e.g. Mepps).
3. You don't need a leader for trout, but one is necessary for northern pike and walleyes.

4. The best fishing is often at the bottom of a rapid or falls, where the fish wait for something edible to flow past. Northern pike like reedy areas.

5. A short collapsible pole and spinning reel are adequate. I've never seen anyone catch anything fly-fishing! On a trip down the Pukaskwa, Ontario, an expert fly fisherman was completely frustrated watching the rest of us, including me, catch brook trout one after another on spoons while he never got a bite on a fly. After cleaning a trout he decided that the trout were feeding on crayfish.

Preparing fish for eating

Fish can be cleaned, filleted, and skinned on a canoe paddle. The offal should be thrown back into the lake or river. At first I thought that this was a bad procedure but then it

High winds bending trees on an island in Georgian Bay, Ontario.

was pointed out to me that sea gulls or other fish will eat the offal and that if it were disposed of on land, it would attract bears. Trout and arctic char don't need skinning because they have no scales. All fried fish taste excellent. Some people prefer frying fish covered with corn meal but fresh fish taste great fried in any manner. After it is gutted, a small brook trout can be cooked on a stick over the fire just like a hot dog. Fish chowder can be a pleasant change from frying.

All fresh water fish caught in Canadian waters should be thoroughly cooked. Otherwise one risks getting fish worms. Although being infected is not a serious health hazard, it is certainly unpleasant. I had this problem after eating an undercooked trout on the Rupert River, Quebec.

Walleyes

Walleyes belong to the perch family. They are so named because of the pearly appearance of the eyes, which have a light-gathering layer that allows them to see in murky water. Canadians call them pickerel, but they are not in the pickerel family. They grow up to 25 inches (65 cm) in length, though most are shorter. A typical weight is one to two pounds. Their bodies are torpedo-shaped and colored olive-brown to golden with a white underside. Walleyes have two distinct back fins. Their life span is about seven years.

Young walleyes eat insects but as they grow older they feed mainly on other fish, feeding in shallow water at dawn and dusk. Northern pike are their primary predators. Walleyes are among the most popular fish and are considered an excellent fish to eat.

Northern pike

"Northerns" like weedy, sheltered places. They wait under cover to ambush other fish. Fancy lures are not required if they are biting. Northerns have an extra set of bones that makes cleaning and filleting difficult. The best northerns are the biggest ones because one can get a knife easily between the sets of bones. Although northerns have a reputation for not tasting as good as walleyes, this is undeserved. On one trip a colleague claimed that northerns weren't worth eating. To test his assertion, we fried pieces of walleye and northern in the same pan and he couldn't tell the difference.

Because northerns are ferocious fighters, they are a lot of fun to catch. They are relatively easy to hook but put up a strong fight. They can grow to be quite large; two to five pounds is not uncommon. Their diet consists mainly of other fish. Large ones will sometimes seize a smaller one that has been hooked, so the fisherman may find he is catching two fish at once. I saw this happen on the Rupert River. My friend Bob hooked a small northern. While he was reeling it in, a large northern bit into the one on the hook and held on even after it was landed. Bob unhooked the smaller one and threw the two of them back into the river. As we watched, the smaller one finally wriggled free from the larger one and swam off.

Gloves and long-nose pliers are recommended for removing lures from the mouths of northerns because they tend to swallow lures and their teeth are sharp. Having band-aids packed with the fishing gear is a good idea … just in case.

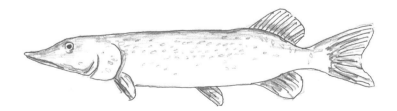

Other fish

Lake trout prefer cool, oxygen-rich water, 40° to 50° F. In summer they often go deep to find cool water. Trolling with spoons or minnow-shaped lures is recommended. The depth depends on the time of the year.

Trout, like salmon and char, have no scales so they don't need to be skinned or scaled. They are excellent eating and the flesh may have a pinkish color.

Brook trout like cold, oxygen-rich water. Therefore they are found in fast flowing streams. Small spinners like Mepps are good lures. Leaders are not needed and they tend to spook trout. Trout often stay at the base of rapids and falls. They are easily spooked so a fishing spot should be approached from downstream. Trout should be handled with wet hands to avoid damage to their sensitive skin. I've heard that there are no trout where there are northern pike.

Arctic char, like trout, are members of the salmon family. They usually weigh between two and five pounds (1 to 2.5 kg). Their flesh ranges from light pink to bright red. They are found in rivers flowing into the Arctic Ocean. They are excellent eating.

There are both **smallmouth and largemouth bass**. Smallmouth bass are probably the feistiest fish of that size. They like steep rock ledges in contrast to largemouth bass, which like weedy areas. The best bait for smallmouth bass are minnow-shaped lures.

Sturgeons are large (they can be 7 to 12 feet long) slow-growing bottom feeders. I have seen sturgeon breeding in shallows of the Missinaibi and Rupert rivers with their tail fins sticking up above the water. On the Rupert, my paddling mate and I cooperated to catch one. He stepped into the shallow water, grabbed a sturgeon near the tail and heaved it onto shore where I waited with a boulder to kill it. Although he deliberately chose the smallest one he could see, it must have weighed over 15 pounds. It fed us for two days. The flesh tasted more like pork than other fish. Our fishing technique was probably illegal and possibly out of season, but with the damming of the Rupert about to happen, we felt no guilt.

Fish Stories

There are many a fish tale that I witnessed that I must relate. Wendell, who was an avid fisherman, tried to cast into a small stream. Unfortunately his lure landed in a tree on the opposite bank. While he was debating what to do, a duck flying upstream hit the line and dislodged the lure. This is true.

Another story involved a priest who caught enough fish to feed his parish, often bringing in a haul when no one else could catch a single fish. One member of his congregation, who happened to work for the Department of Natural Resources, was very eager to learn the priest's secret. After promising never to tell the priest's secret fishing methods to anyone, the young man finally persuaded the priest to let him accompany him fishing. When they were in the middle of the lake, the priest opened his tackle box and took out a half stick of dynamite, which he lit and threw into the lake. After the explosion, he scooped up the fish that had floated to the surface. His companion protested and said he'd have to report this illegal fishing to the DNR, whereupon he was reminded of his oath not to tell a soul. While he was still sputtering, the priest took out the other half stick of dynamite, lit it, and handed it to him, saying,

Rocky Defile on the Coppermine River, Nunavut.

"Now you fish or cut bait." While this story may not be true, I remember being camped one night on the shores of Lake Mistassani, Quebec, hearing explosions and finally realizing that it was the local Cree fishing with dynamite.

Other leisure activities

Dirty laundry accumulates during a long trip, and a leisure day offers an opportunity to clean up. Washing can be done in a river or lake, but if one has concerns about polluting the water, one may do laundry in one of the larger cooking pots. Painters can be used as laundry lines. When wet wool is hung, the wetness drains to the lowest spot. Drying can be hastened by wringing the lowest spots some time after hanging.

Many people like to hike. After sitting for days, it feels great to unbend the legs. Good hiking boots are a necessity for navigating wet places, rocky slopes, and long distances. Bring along a compass so you don't get lost. North of the tree line, distances are deceiving because there are no trees as references. A hill that appears to be a mile away may actually be five miles away. Hiking offers an opportunity to observe animals. Many animals of the north are described in Appendix 9.

Modern cameras are so lightweight that there is little excuse for not carrying one. Often the most interesting pictures are not of scenery, but of tiny flowers, lichen, and rocks. I have often been disappointed with pictures of wildlife, because in the pictures the animals look so small. For wildlife photography, one really needs a telephoto lens. Bird watching is another activity that some enjoy.

Many of us try to keep a journal of our trips. It requires a great deal of self-discipline. I often let a day or two slide and then each day seems to blur into another. A nice alternative is to have a common journal for the whole party. Each day a different person enters the log, and the next morning reads what he or she wrote. This not only spreads the job around, but also gives varied perspectives.

I also like to swim whenever the air temperature isn't freezing. It's a good way to get clean.

A layover day is a good time to read a novel that one can't find the time to read at home. I find particularly interesting the stories of early adventurers who traveled the same river. It's fun to relate these stories to what one sees today. Fossicking, or prospecting, is another leisure activity. For several years I searched riverbanks for a black pebble, with a perfectly perpendicular white cross intrusion. After finding one, I made it into a pendant on a chain for my wife.

I always enjoy something to sit on. I need to for painting, but I also enjoy sitting while I'm eating, reading, or just chatting around the fire. I remember participating in contests over the best spot. I finally began to carry my own chair.

Weather

Weather patterns

In trying to understand and predict wind directions, it should be remembered that in North America the prevailing weather comes from the west, but the weather doesn't always follow this pattern. Winds tend to blow clockwise around high-pressure cells and counterclockwise around lows. As a high-pressure cell approaches from the west, winds first will bring cold air from the north. Then as the cell passes, the winds will shift to warm southerly air. If the center of the cell passes north of the observer, there will be a period of easterly winds.

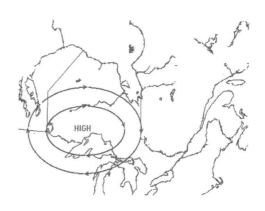

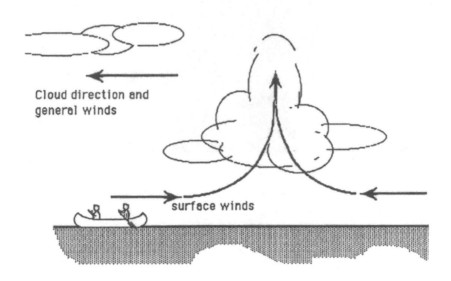

Cloud direction and
general winds

surface winds

If it passes to the south, the winds will be westerly. Counter-clockwise winds around a low-pressure cell have the opposite effect. There are warm south winds as the low approaches and cold north winds as it leaves.

Often the wind direction at water level doesn't correlate with the motion of the clouds. This may be the result of local thermal effects. An updraft associated with an approaching thunderhead may draw surface air toward it, so the surface winds may blow in a direction opposite to high level winds. In fact, observation of this phenomenon may foretell the arrival of severe weather.

Rain

There is no point in remaining in the sack if it's raining in the morning. Staying in the tent because of rain will make you miserable and bored. It's much better to get out, take down the tent, and start the day. The tent can be dried when it is put up at night. Layover days should be saved for nice weather. Paddling in the rain is tolerable provided one has adequate rain gear, there is no threat of lightning, and there aren't strong headwinds. Hot lunches revive spirits on rainy days, as does the rainbow that frequently appears after a rain storm.

Snow and ice

Snow is possible in northern Ontario even in the middle of May. It always comes as a surprise, but it needn't hamper travel. Spruce branches make nice brooms for sweeping snow off tents. Ice on the tent must be melted before the tent is folded. Finding loose gear under snow can take more than the usual amount of searching.

On an early trip, ice may be on large lakes. If it is solid, it can cause delays. One year, we started a trip on Lake Mistassani in Quebec. The outlet to the Rupert River, Quebec, was ten miles across the lake, which was half covered with ice. Rather than risk being stuck in the middle of the lake, we hired a local Cree to tow our two canoes across the lake behind his motorized canoe. The waves created by passing through a number of patches of rotten ice caused the vertical columnar crystals to separate. As they fell on each other, there was the sound of tinkling bells—a beautiful and most unnatural sound.

Later, on the river, we saw a white beach, which turned out to be pure snowy ice.

In early spring trips one may encounter blocks of ice on the shore. During spring trips, ice for drinks can often be found in shaded north exposures. When ice breaks up on large rivers, great ice piles form at certain places.[1] These can last well into June. I remember seeing a large white object miles ahead on the Moose River, Ontario. It turned out to be an eight-foot-tall block of ice on an island. Along the river, ice moving downstream during break-up had completely flattened stands of small trees.

---

1   The original meaning of the word *debacle* is the breaking up of river ice.

Headwinds

Every time I've been on a river that flows into James Bay or Hudson Bay, I have encountered headwinds. They develop in late morning and grow in intensity during the afternoon. Only after sunset do they die down. They are much more intense on sunny days. They are caused by the sun heating the air over the forests. As the heated air rises, it draws in colder air from the bay. It's very discouraging to paddle against these winds. They can send a canoe upstream against the current. The best way to avoid them is to make a very early start and quit mid-afternoon. We did this on the Fawn and Severn rivers in Ontario. Every morning we would pass another party still sacked in. As darkness fell, they would pass us, long after we had made camp. I wondered how they made camp in the dark.

When there is a headwind on a river, each bend ahead offers hope of relief. Usually, however, the wind direction changes so it is still a headwind. On the North French, Ontario, the headwinds near the bay were so strong that we were forced to tow the canoe from shore.

Sometimes one may be wind-bound on a large lake because the wind is so fierce that it just doesn't pay to paddle. On Lake Superior, I've had to quit paddling in the early afternoon because the waves were too high to brave. Appendix 7 discusses waves. Sun-caused winds start blowing on the same schedule every day. On a large lake strong winds create large waves. Overcast days are usually calm. Wind-bound days can be used for hiking the surrounding area, or alternatively, for fishing, reading, painting, photography, and general cleaning up. When a trip involves big lakes, it pays to allow an extra day or two for such contingencies.

Several times heavy headwinds have made daytime paddling impossible so headway became possible only by paddling at night when the wind had dropped. One such experience was on a trip down the Fond du Lac River where it empties into Black Lake in Saskatchewan. Our group was held up at a campsite for a day and a half. Finally at 12:30 a.m. in the second night, one of our party woke everyone to report that the wind had finally died and the water was calm. Within a half hour, our tents were down and the canoes loaded. Fortunately there was enough moonlight to navigate by keeping the lakeshore visible on our left. It was a magical paddle. Moonlight sparkled on the water and the display of northern lights on our right was wonderful. After a few hours the sun began to rise behind us. At six we stopped for a breakfast break having covered 19 miles (30 km). Another similar experience occurred on Beverly Lake on the Thelon River, Nunavut. As we paddled through the night, the glow of sunset in the north gradually turned into a sunrise.

Early morning mist can make beautiful photographs or paintings, especially if the mist silhouettes the trees. Morning mist is most common in late summer or early fall, when the water is warmer than the air above it. Late risers miss this visual treat.

Weather changes: Superstitions and Omens

When an expedition is underway and the first signs of a drizzle occur, there is a great reluctance to break out and don rain gear. Many of us have a deep-rooted superstition that if enough people put on rain gear, the rain will stop. We hate to put on rain gear and then take it off so we look to the other members of the party to stop the rain by donning their own gear.

After several trips, I've come to wonder if what people say can affect the weather. Once, on the Pukaskwa, Ontario, during a heavy plague of black flies, my partner said, "What we need is some cold weather to keep the bugs down." The next night, as he lay shivering in his sleeping bag and there was freezing rain outside, he said, "I'd even take black flies if I could get warm." Within two days, we had very warm weather again with black flies. Another year I paddled the same river with his son who had lived in California for eight years. As he was telling us how good it felt to be in forests, he mentioned that he missed thunderstorms. Within two hours we had a storm so violent that it put out our campfire.

One old saying that seems to be reliable is, "red sky at night, sailors' delight; red sky in the morning, sailors take warning." Also, "ring around the moon" and "mare's tail" clouds (wispy cirrus clouds composed of ice crystals that appear as veil patches or strands) may signal bad weather.

Strong winds can lift tents and blow them considerable distances. It is wise to stake a tent as soon as it has been erected and fill it with gear or even a heavy rock. Canoes should be tied to a tree or heavy rock. My buddies tell of an incident on a trip down the Winisk River, Ontario. They had spread wet clothing on a rock ledge to dry after a swim. Suddenly a squall came through and blew things around. They saw a large spruce lean so far that its roots lifted. A bathing suit was blown under the tree. When the tree righted itself, they could not tip the tree enough to pull the suit out. That bathing suit was lost forever.

Though a steady breeze can be annoying, a light breeze is cherished when it keeps the black flies and mosquitoes away. At such times a breezy campsite is sought instead of a sheltered one.

Sun

On sunny days, skin and eye protection may be required to prevent overexposure. The problem is magnified on the water because of the reflection. Often thin clouds may falsely lead to complacency about the sun. Dark glasses, a hat, long sleeves, and sunburn lotion will help prevent sunburn. I've had a particular problem with the back of my hands hardening and splitting. A&D ointment helps.

Canoes and Paddles

A brief history of canoes

North American natives used birch-bark canoes for many centuries before the European invasion. The frames were made of cedar. Bark was sewn together with tree roots and sealed with resin. The fur-trading voyageurs used birch bark canoes of several different sizes. For paddling from Montreal through the Great Lakes, they used the *canot de M'atre*, which was about 36 feet long with a 6-foot beam and weighed about 600 pounds. The crew consisted of 6 to 12 people, 8 to 10 being normal. It was portaged by four men and had a capacity of 6,000 pounds consisting of 65 bundles (piéces) of fur, each weighing 90 pounds, plus the crew and their personal gear. The *canot du Nord* was somewhat shorter and better adapted to river travel. It was used on rivers and lakes north and west of the Great Lakes. Its length was about 25 feet, was 4 to 4.5 feet abeam and weighed 300 pounds. It had a crew of 4 to 8 men and was portaged by two. Its capacity was 3,000 pounds plus crew and personal gear. A mid-sized canoe, *canot batard*, was used for transporting dignitaries and messages.

Advertisements for Old Town and Peterborough Canoes.

The first canvas-covered wood canoes appeared in the nineteenth century. The hull of cedar ribs and planks was covered with canvas, and then it was filled with white lead and painted. The manufacture of wood-and-canvas canoes began around Peterborough, Ontario, about 1860. In 1892 the Peterborough Canoe Company produced five styles of canoes. In 1923 a joint holding company was formed with the Chestnut Canoe Company of New Brunswick. The Peterborough Company went bankrupt in 1962 and the Chestnut Canoe Company followed in 1974. The Old Town Canoe Company in Maine started making wood and canvas canoes in 1900. The Old Town, Peterborough, and Chestnut canoe companies were the dominant canoe makers until after World War II when other materials began to replace the wood and canvas canoes.

The Grumman Aircraft Company produced the first aluminum canoes in 1944. These canoes were lighter and stronger than wood-and-canvas ones. Somewhat later, other companies began making canoes of resin-bonded fiberglass. As soon as DuPont marketed Kevlar® fibers in the 1970s, these began to replace glass fibers because of their lighter weight and greater strength. In the 1960s, the U.S. Rubber Company introduced a foamed ABS under the trade name Royalite™. Later polyethylene has found its way into the canoe market.

Size, weight, and buoyancy considerations

Commercially available canoes vary with respect to size, material, and general design. The length of a canoe governs how fast it can be paddled and how quickly it can be turned. Naval architects have proven that when boats of the same general shape are propelled with the same force, the velocity increases with the square root of the length—shorter boats are slower. For wilderness travel, a length of about 17 feet is reasonable. Shorter canoes have less carrying capacity and are slower. Longer canoes are heavier, more cumbersome to portage, and harder to maneuver in rivers.

The weight of a canoe is important on any trip that involves portaging. Light canoes are easier to carry. Most canoes have a center thwart at the balance point. This is essential for easy carrying. On one trip, a colleague had a heavy fiberglass canoe without a center thwart. He had to carry it by balancing the floor of the canoe on his head. This obstructed the view ahead and was painful.

Another crucial consideration is the buoyancy of the canoe when it is filled with water. While we don't like to think of capsizes, a canoe's behavior after a capsize is important. Most canoes have buoyancy compartments in the bow and stern filled with foam. These are not necessary for wood/canvas or foamed ABS canoes. Auxiliary inflatable flotation can be lashed into canoes to increase their buoyancy and is often used in white water. One of its advantages is that it also displaces water in the event of a capsize, making it less likely that the canoe will wrap around rocks.

Canoe materials

Wood and canvas canoes are heavy, easily damaged and tend to gain weight during a trip because wood absorbs water. Their main appeal is aesthetic.

Two different aluminum alloys are used for canoes. Grumman uses 0.062 inch-thick sheets of aluminum alloy 6061. These sheets are stamped into two symmetric canoe halves, which are then heat-treated to a T-6 temper that combines the hardening effects of the stamping and the heat treatment. Most other brands of aluminum canoes are made from aluminum alloy 5052, which is not heat-treatable and not as strong. Its strength is obtained during cold rolling and stamping of the sheet. Canoe halves in both cases are riveted together.

ABS is an acrylonitrile-butadiene-styrene copolymer. Laminated sheets are sold under the trade name, Rolayex™. These sheets are composed of a foamable ABS core surrounded by several layers of ABS substrate and covered by a vinyl skin. The basic laminate can be altered for critical areas by changing the number of layers of ABS or even the foamable ABS core. The laminated sheet is heated in an oven, which causes the core to expand into a closed-cell foam and make the other layers soft enough for forming. The laminate is then placed in a heated mold and vacuum formed into the shape of the hull.

Because ABS is a thermoplastic, dents can be removed by heating with boiling water or back in civilization with a hot air dryer. Polymers are poor conductors of heat, so it takes a while to heat through. The temptation to hurry the process by increasing the temperature of the blower should be resisted because the skin can be overheated.

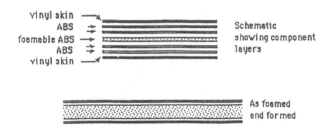

vinyl skin
ABS
foamable ABS
ABS
vinyl skin

Schematic showing component layers

As foamed and formed

Today some canoes are made from molded polyethylene. The very low stiffness of polyethylene can be overcome by either using a foamed core (like ABS) or with aluminum gunwales and keel.

There are several systems of fiber-reinforced composites. The cheaper ones are made from polyester resin reinforced with fiberglass. Lighter composite canoes are made from epoxy reinforced with Kevlar® or carbon fibers. These composites may be made by using fibers in the form of woven cloth or a mat. Composites lend themselves to sharper bows than are possible with aluminum, ABS, or polyethylene.

The properties of several materials used in canoes are listed in the table below.

Density, Stiffness, and Strength of Canoe Materials[1]

Material	Density g/cm^3	Elastic modulus 10^6 psi	Tensile strength 10^3 psi
Kevlar® 49 fiber	1.44	18.0	400
E-glass fibers	2.55	11.0	220
S-glass	2.49	12.5	275
Polyester resin	1.14	low	low
Epoxy resin	1.20	low	low
Aluminum	2.70	10.0	42[2], 38[3]
ABS	1.05	low	low
High density polyethylene	0.96	low	depends[4]
Carbon fiber	2.25	30 to 100	300 to 1000
Wood	0.90	0.8	7

1   Calculated assuming a woven cloth constructed with a typical volume fraction of fiber (50%) so the combined densities are the average of the fiber and matrix and the composite strength and stiffness is about ¼ of that of the fiber.
2   Al 6061-T6
3   Al 5052-H34
4   The strength of polyethylene depends strongly on the degree of molecular orientation.

The basic construction methods used for fiberglass and Kevlar® canoes are similar. Layers of woven cloth of fiberglass or Kevlar® are bonded with a suitable plastic resin, usually polyester for fiberglass and epoxy for Kevlar®. With both materials, the high strength fibers account for about 50% by volume, the other 50% being the resin. Because the layers of cloth are laid up by hand, extra material can be added in critical areas. The molds are much less expensive than those used for stamping aluminum or for vacuum molding ABS or polyethylene. The ability to form sharp curves has permitted new hull shapes in fiberglass and Kevlar®. It should be noted that some fiberglass canoes are made with mats of fiberglass rather than woven cloth and some cheaper canoes are made by blowing chopped fibers into the mold. These are not as strong for the same weight as those made from woven fabric.

Glass fibers are made from E-glass, which is very similar in composition to glass for windows and bottles. The high strength of fibers is attributable to their very small size (typically about 0.0009 inches in diameter.) Small diameter fibers can carry more force per cross-sectional area because of fewer defects than are found in larger cross sections. Kevlar® 49 is an aramid in which the long chain molecules have been aligned.[5] A typical diameter is about 0.0004 inches. Kevlar's high strength and low density has led to its use in aerospace applications and bulletproof vests. These same properties have allowed Kevlar® canoes to be much lighter than fiberglass ones. More recently canoes have been made with carbon-fiber reinforcement. Carbon fibers are stronger than Kevlar® but are more brittle so carbon-fiber canoes are used principally for flat-water racing canoes.

---

5   Polyethylene has the simplest structure of all polymers. It is composed of very long molecules having a carbon-carbon backbone with two hydrogen atoms attached to each carbon atom. These are essentially the same molecules as in kerosene, gasoline, Vaseline grease, and paraffin wax except that they are much longer.

Relative costs

The cost of a new canoe varies with the material. The rough price range relative to fiber glass canoes are approximately:

Fiberglass	1.0
Polyethylene	~ 1.0
Aluminum	1.0 to 1.25
Royalex (ABS)	1.3 to 1.9
Kevlar	2.0 to 2.5
Graphite fiber	3.5
Wood & canvas	~ 10.0

Effect of canoe material

One of the key elements in canoe design is the stiffness of the hull. A certain amount of hull flexibility is desirable, because it allows the canoe to squeeze between rocks. Too much flexibility, however, will allow the bottom to "oil can"— in which the bottom elastically springs upward into a different shape. Oil canning is very annoying in open water and slows the canoe. The stiffness of sheet materials depend on their elastic moduli and their thicknesses. Of the canoe materials, aluminum has the greatest stiffness. Hulls of other materials need to be considerably thicker. The fibers in fiberglass, Kevlar, and carbon composites provide the stiffness. ABS and polyethylene have very low stiffness. The use of foamed laminates takes advantage of the fact that when an object is bent, most of the stress is carried by the outer fibers. Foaming the core displaces the denser material outward, creating an effective thickness much greater than a solid sheet of the same material. The same underlying principle is the basis for using I-beams in construction instead of solid bars.

Midnight at Bathurst Inlet in Nunavut.

The big advantage of aluminum canoes is that they are more rugged than others. They will dent, but dents can be pounded out. Other materials tend to tear, and tears are far more serious than dents. The same abuse can cause much deeper scratches on other canoes. Aluminum canoes, unlike canoes made from other materials, can be stored outside without deterioration from sunlight.

Aluminum canoes have several disadvantages. They are noisy, they are cold, and they tend to cling to any rocks that they scrape. The noise generated by contact with paddles, from waves and from scraping against rocks is an affront to the stillness of the wilderness. An approaching aluminum canoe can be heard many minutes before the canoe is seen, whereas ABS and composite canoes can sneak up noiselessly if the paddlers aren't talking. The high thermal conductivity of aluminum produces a cold seat and knees when paddling in cold water. A companion of mine resorted to lining his seat with moss while paddling on Lake Superior. The tendency to cling to rocks is a serious problem while running rapids. The side of a canoe that brushes against a rock is slowed down so the current tends to turn the canoe. This causes further problems. Again and again, I have noted aluminum canoes fall far behind the others in a rocky stretch of river.

Fiberglass canoes, while strong, suffer from lack of toughness or the ability to absorb energy without breaking. Another disadvantage is weight. Although the density of fiberglass composite is 1.84 in comparison to 2.7 for aluminum, its lower stiffness requires a greater thickness. This in turn means that fiberglass canoes must be either heavier or have lower gunwales than aluminum ones. Their advantages include: low cost, quiet, do not conduct heat, do not stick to rocks, and refined hull shapes make paddling and maneuvering easier.

Kevlar® overcomes the weight problem of fiberglass. The lower density and greater stiffness allow Kevlar® canoes to be considerably lighter than all others except carbon-fiber canoes. The big disadvantage is the high cost.

The disadvantages of ABS include weight and the inability to vacuum form highly refined hull shapes. Because of their blunt entry lines, ABS canoes require greater effort to propel than canoes made of fiberglass or Kevlar®.

Aluminum also suffers from this to some degree, although the high bow offers some safety in standing waves so there is a compromise. ABS and polyethylene canoes are extremely flexible. They will spring back after having been bent.

Hull shape

The shape of the bow has a large effect on how much effort is required to propel a canoe. In general, a bow that is sharp and relatively steep, like that of an ocean liner, cuts through the water with less resistance than a bow that enters the water at a low angle like the classic birch bark and canvas covered wooden canoes.

Before buying my Mad River Explorer, my wife and I tried it out in a pond. After noting how fast we passed floating objects, I remarked, "We're really zipping along." My wife in the bow replied, "No, we can't be going very fast. I can hear it when we do." She was used to hearing the bow wave in our Grumman canoe; the Mad River Explorer's steep hull shape allowed us to slip easily and quietly through the water.

Stuart Cohen and I tested three canoes in the University of Michigan naval tow tank.[6] One was the 16.5-foot Kevlar® Mad River Explorer and the other two were 17-foot Grummans. One of the Grummans was new and the bottom of the other had severe dents. Each canoe was loaded with 500 pounds to simulate the weight of two people and gear. Tests were made at different speeds. The finite size of the tow tank caused a little extra drag, so the measured forces were corrected to what they would be in open water. The following graph shows how the resistance varied with speed. The measurements for two Grumman canoes were almost identical, which indicates that the dented bottom had no appreciable effect. The resistance of the Mad River canoe was much lower because of the bow shape.

---

6   William Hosford and Stuart Cohen, "The Resistance of Canoes," *Nastawgan, Quarterly Journal of the Wilderness Canoe Association*, Vol. 21, No. 2 (Summer 1994), pp. 20-21.

*Eleven o'clock at night on the South Nahanni River,
Northwest Territories.*

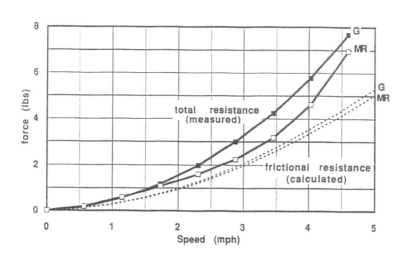

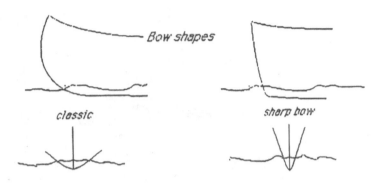

Bow waves also depend on the length of a canoe. It surprises many people to learn that the longer the canoe, the lower the drag. The residual resistance of a 16-foot canoe is 3% greater than for a 17-foot canoe.

Canoes also differ in the shape of their hull as seen from above. The gunwale of the traditional hull is gradually curved from the bow to the stern. Recently tapered hulls have been introduced. For the same length and beam, they glide more easily through the water but lack a bit in carrying capacity.

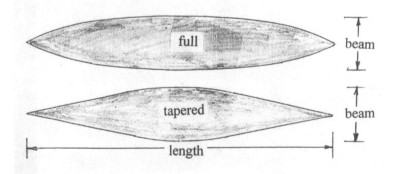

The shape of the bottom is also of interest. A flat bottom has more initial stability than a curved or V-shaped one and draws less water for the same load. However a flat bottom has a lower final stability, which can lead to a sudden capsizing. This is because as the canoe tips, a flat bottom canoe has less contact with the water than a canoe with a round bottom.

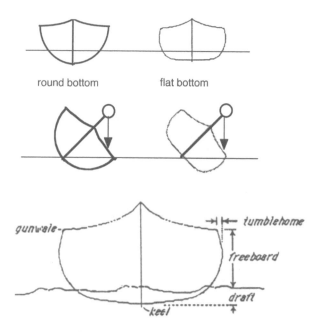

round bottom   flat bottom

gunwale — tumblehome

freeboard

draft

keel

"Tumblehome" is the inward curvature of the sides. It serves to stiffen the sides and decrease the distance one must reach outward to paddle.

Depth is the distance between the bottom and a line between the gunwales at the canoe's middle. With insufficient depth, waves are likely to pour over the gunwales in rough water. Depth of 12.5 inches is sufficient in calm water, but a greater depth is desirable for running rapids. A canoe's carrying capacity increases with depth.

The beam is the width at the maximum point. The beam at the waterline controls the ease of paddling. A canoe with a narrower waterline beam is faster. Racing canoes have a 27-inch beam at a 3-inch waterline. However, for wilderness canoe tripping, a wider beam provides more carrying capacity. A waterline beam of 32 inches at the 4-inch is good.

A keel attached to the bottom serves to keep a canoe on a straight course in flat water. It also stiffens the bottom. However a keel tends to catch on rocks in rapids. V-bottoms

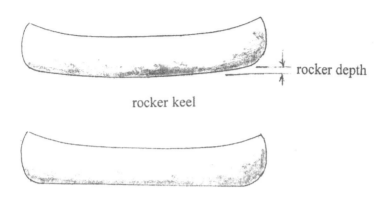

rocker depth

rocker keel

straight line keel

can provide some tracking ability without a keel. The shape of the keel line may be either straight or curved upward at bow and stern. The latter is called a rocker bottom. Most canoes have some rocker to allow them to turn easily. A rocker depth of 1.5 inches will allow the canoe to turn easily in rapids and rise with waves. Canoes used in white water usually have extreme rocker while canoes primarily for lake travel have very little. A half-inch rocker is sufficient for flat-water paddling and no rocker is desirable for racing.

While a large capacity is advantageous for carrying equipment, a canoe with a large capacity is usually a slow canoe. Advertised capacities have little meaning because different manufactures use different criteria. A light canoe is desirable for portaging. However the weight of a canoe depends on the depth, length, and beam, as well as its construction materials. Gaining lightness by having lower gunnels and thinner gauge material is bad.

Skimping of thickness and material can decrease weight but at the expense of strength. Aluminum canoes have superior abrasion resistance. Royalex, polyethylene, and ABS are better than fiberglass. Canvas-covered wood canoes are least durable.

Gunwales are usually made of wood or aluminum, even if the canoe is made from a polymeric material. I find wooden gunwales more aesthetic. Because of the construction of old wood and canvas canoes, there were open slots between the ribs. These slots are handy for tying things and make it easier to drain a canoe by tipping. A few modern canoes have incorporated this feature by slotting the inwales.

Modifications

In white water, impacting rocks may damage the bow. Damaged bows can be reinforced with a *shoe,* which is an extra layer of fiberglass or Kevlar®. Shoes also protect the bow when landing on sandy or rocky shores. One need not wait for damage to apply a shoe.

D-rings that attach to the bottom of a canoe are convenient for lashing packs. One advantage of lashing packs to the bottom instead of tying them to thwarts is that in the event of swamping they will provide buoyancy. Also, packs lashed tightly to the bottom of a canoe will help right the canoe after an upset because the center of gravity will be above the waterline when the canoe is upside down. On one trip I saw my daughter's canoe float upside-down while she was lining it. Then the canoe righted itself because her packs were tied to the bottom. At the end of the lining she had only a quart of water to bail.

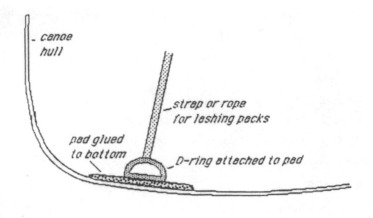

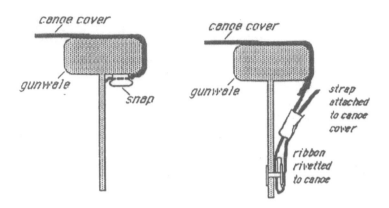

Canoe covers will help prevent swamping in heavy waves by shedding water. Whether it is desirable to have them cover the whole canoe or only the cargo region depends on the nature of the water. Full covers provide more protection but cause more difficulty in loading and unloading, and they are also heavier to portage.

There are at least two ways of attaching a canoe cover. One is simply to use snaps. These may be screwed to the underside of the gunwale or the outside of the canoe body. The other system involves tying the cover to a long webbed ribbon permanently attached to the outside of the canoe by rivets.

Canoe repair in the bush

A canoe repair kit is worth packing. Duct tape, black electricians' tape, and bathtub caulk are useful for leaks. Gorilla glue is especially strong. With an aluminum canoe, machine screws and nuts can replace rivets. Steel screws are adequate for the duration of a trip, but should be replaced by aluminum rivets afterward. Wire has a variety of uses. It can be used to splint a broken thwart with a spruce branch or to repair seats. Broken paddles can be glued with epoxy and reinforced with duct tape or wire. Pliers and a screwdriver are useful. A Swiss army knife with an awl can be used to make holes for wire binding. Dents in aluminum canoes can be taken out by jumping on the inside. Hot water with a little pressure is needed for ABS.

Abandoning a canoe

On some trips it is not economical to fly a canoe back out at the end. For such trips the selection of the canoe will be strongly influenced by the price. If one can buy an old aluminum canoe for $200, then abandoning it or selling it to the local inhabitants for $100 is cheaper than flying it home for $800. Twice on trips ending at Severn and Winisk on Hudson Bay, my colleagues and I have done exactly that.

Paddles

All of the force exerted by the paddle goes into propelling the canoe, regardless of the shape of the paddle. As odd as it may seem, a round tree limb used as a paddle is as effective in transmitting force as a paddle of the most sophisticated design. However the paddle shape strongly influences how effectively the power of the paddler is converted to propelling the canoe. The power expended by the paddler is the force times the velocity that the paddle moves relative to the water. A narrow paddle must be moved through the water faster than a wide paddle to achieve the same force.

A good paddle design minimizes the weight of the paddle, decreases the air resistance on the return forward and makes steering easy. The reason why the weight of a paddle is important is that if a person paddles for eight hours and lifts the paddle 1,500 times, a one-ounce decrease in the paddle weight means that the person will lift 930 pounds less.

There are many designs of paddles. They come in different lengths, ranging from 54 to 70 inches. The longer the paddle is, the more leverage one can get, but at a greater force. In the past it has been recommended that the paddle should be long enough to reach the armpits. However, this ignores the height of seats and the position of the paddler (sitting or kneeling, bow or stern). The length should be such that one hand can comfortably grip the shaft just above the blade (at the balance point) and hold it just above water level while the other hand is almost parallel with the shoulders. Because the bow seat is usually lower than the stern seat, the bow paddle should be shorter.

Wooden paddles are usually made of spruce, maple, or ash. Soft woods (spruce) tend to be lighter than hard woods (maple or ash). Often paddles are laminated. Reasonably priced paddles with an aluminum shaft and polyethylene blades have become common. They are quite satisfactory but the round shafts tend to roll on the gunwale and the aluminum is cold to hold. Very recently some very light shafts have been made from graphite.

There are a variety of grips. The *pear* grip is traditional, but in recent years *T-handle* grips have gained popularity. I find the pear grip more comfortable, but I can grip the T-handle more firmly, so I use a compromise, which I carve from a pear grip. A commercial handle can be modified with a rasp and sandpaper.

pear grip   *T-handle*   *compromise*

Traditionally the blade width was about six inches, but now blades eight or ten inches wide are available. I prefer a wider blade because fewer strokes are needed for the same propulsion. Today most paddles are of laminated construction, which leads to more consistent strength.

Blades vary in area from about 115 to 165 square inches. A 6-inch by 26-inch blade has an area of 156 square inches. Paddles with larger blades are useful in white water but smaller blades are preferable for long-distance paddling. The edge of the blade should be thin enough to cut easily through the water but not so thin as to be easily damaged. A thickness of 3/32 inch is about right for paddling.

A recent innovation is the bent shaft blade. They are more efficient for racing because the blade is held perpendicular to the water for a greater portion of the stroke. I regard them with suspicion for ordinary touring or running rapids. One must be constantly aware of which side of the blade is facing forward. Steering must be accomplished by constant switching of the side on which one is paddling.

Wooden paddles should be finished in varnish or oil.

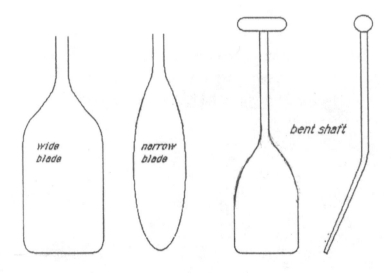

wide blade   narrow blade   bent shaft

Reflections

Memories from canoe trips grow through the winter months and can last for years. Seeing an animal in the wilderness for the first time is a treat. The habits of some of the wild animals of the north are described in Appendix 9. I have a vivid memory of when I first heard a loon. It was in the evening on Rocky Island Lake, Ontario. I thought it was the cry of an insane woman, imagining that she was being attacked. The cry of the loon has since become, to me, a symbol of the north woods. I remember the first time I saw an osprey dive, catch a fish, and swim off with it. I also recall watching a pair of eagles soaring overhead. I recall enjoying an after-dinner drink sitting on a granite ledge overlooking a wild lake when a beaver swam by with a stick in its mouth. I remember watching a herd of 20 to 30 muskoxen grazing near the Coppermine River, Nunavut, before they became aware of us and lumbered away.

One morning on the Missinaibi River, Ontario, I was awakened by what sounded like a jackhammer directly above our tent. It turned out to be a pileated woodpecker. Canada jays are bold enough to steal crumbs and small bits of food while one is still eating. I love to watch sea gulls squabble over fish entrails that we have thrown into the water. Often while paddling down a river a duck will take flight downstream. It will take off and fly farther downstream whenever our canoe approaches it, repeating this many times. I imagine that the duck was trying to lure us away from its ducklings, even when we were so far downstream that we couldn't get back if we had wanted to.

Near-disasters

My first canoe adventure was with two high school buddies. We made a trip on the Delaware River (between New Jersey and Pennsylvania) in an 18-foot wood-and-canvas canoe, starting at Port Jervis with the intention of paddling to Trenton. After two days of fascinating paddling through the Walpack bend and the Delaware Watergap, we camped at Belvidere, just upstream from a rapid. The next morning we tried to cross to the opposite shore before running through the rapid but were sucked downstream faster than we expected and were swept broadside into a rock that punctured a hole in the side of the canoe. A whole day was spent patching the hole with a piece of veneer from a discarded door onto the canoe. However, once the veneer became wet with river water, it expanded, forming ripples that channeled water into the canoe as we paddled on. Because of the leak and then rainy weather, the trip ended at Phillipsburg.

After portaging my gear and life jacket around a short rapid on the Little Missinaibi River, Ontario, I decided to run the canoe empty. All went well initially and I shouted jubilantly as the canoe entered the pool at the bottom. I was rudely surprised as the canoe was swamped by the large waves created where the fast water entered the pool. I had no PFD and foolishly was wearing high hiking boots, which made it difficult to swim to shore.

Still another near-disaster occurred at the bottom of the South Nahanni River, Northwest Territories. The current was carrying us along and all I had to do was steer. It seemed so easy that my bow

Manitou Falls on the Fond du Lac River, Saskatchewan.

partner, with my approval, was painting a picture. Then, before I could react fast enough, our canoe was drawn sideward into a sweeper. Of course we went over. Fortunately another canoe was close and picked us up. A third canoe dragged our canoe to the bank, where we dried out during lunch. If the others had not been there, we would have been in serious trouble.

On one trip with my wife and another couple, we portaged without a trail from Montreal Lake to the upper part of the Batchewana River in Ontario. Once on the Batchewana, we encountered many short portages. Running a short rapid, our early model ABS canoe became pinned broadside against a boulder in the middle of the river and filled with water. My wife and the other couple managed to get all of our gear to shore; however, both gunwales had broken and the canoe had collapsed so that its bottom was against the middle thwart. The canoe seemed completely destroyed and the prospect of extricating the canoe appeared hopeless. However I found that by bending at the knees with my thighs against the canoe and straightening my legs, I could move the canoe, one inch at a time, along the boulder. Eventually the canoe became free and snapped back into its original shape with the splintered gunnels perfectly rejoined.

On the White River, Ontario, I pulled ashore just above a tree that had fallen into the river so I could scout a minor rapid. Once my partner and I decided to run it, we started to paddle upstream before heading into it. However, the current caught the bow and swung it downstream as we pushed off so we broadsided the fallen tree. My partner was able to climb out onto the tree, but my body was swept under the tree and I found myself hanging onto the trunk with one hand. I didn't have enough strength to pull my head above water so that I could breathe. I thought I would drown, but the next thing I knew, I was floating downstream on my back, feet first. I was safe! After climbing out of the water, we unloaded the canoe. Once we had the saw, we cut the tree apart to free the canoe. It had a broken gunwale and the side was pulled away from the center thwart. That evening I cut down a small cedar tree and fashioned a section of gunwale from it. This was attached to the canoe with duct tape and wire.

Complacency can cause problems. I lost my PFD in the first day of a 23-day trip on the Thelon River, Nunavut. The river was flowing slowly and smoothly and our canoe was well ahead of the others. I took off my PFD and put it on the back plate of the canoe so I could lie on it to rest while waiting for the others to catch up. When I finally roused, the PFD was nowhere to be found. We even paddled back looking for it. Without a PFD, I had to be extra careful the rest of the trip.

Near the end of a trip on the Severn River as we approached Hudson Bay, our group pulled to shore to relieve ourselves. There was plenty of current so we didn't consider any tidal action. However, when one of our group turned around, he spotted one of the canoes floating away. It was rescued only after he quickly jumped in the remaining canoe and chased it. Apparently tides can affect the water level well upstream from salt water.

Special places

The Pukaskwa River is a small river flowing from the highlands between Highway 17 and Lake Superior in Ontario. It has enough water to be navigable only in the spring. It drops about 600 feet (180 m) in about 60 miles (100 km) and is filled with brook trout. Even I, a non-fisherman, was able to catch one whenever I tried. One of the most spectacular places is where the whole river flows between rock banks only six feet (two meters) apart. One can reach out and touch both banks at the same time. The current at this spot isn't very fast, which means the river must be very deep. My friend says the river turns on its side here. After the Pukaskwa empties into Lake Superior, there is either a 50-mile (80 km) paddle to the east to Michicopoten or a 50-mile (80 km) paddle to the west to Heron Bay, Ontario. In either case, the lakeshore landscape is breathtaking.

Waterfalls are always spectacular. The Virginia Falls on the Nahanni River, Northwest Territories, is a world heritage site. The total drop is about twice as high as Niagara. Although the amount of water is much less, it is a huge fall. Lesser falls on the Rupert (Quebec), Missinaibi (Ontario), Pukaskwa (Ontario), Ground Hog, and Fond du Lac (Saskatchewan) are awe-inspiring. The views from mountains also make wonderful pictures.

One of my most spectacular campsites was on the Missinaibi, halfway between Missinaibi Lake and Highway 11. Three falls are close together. We camped just above the second falls where we could enjoy the roar of the water and see both of the other two falls. The campsite had a flat ledge of clean rock for our tents and fire.

Another memorable campsite was on the Rupert River. At least an acre was absolutely flat and bare except for caribou

moss under scattered trees. We had no problem finding a place to put up a tent. The only problem was the danger of the dry moss catching fire so we made our fire near the river, well away from the tent area.

There is a very special place on the Mountain River, Northwest Territories. We were told that there was a natural bridge back from the river near First Canyon. We were amazed as we realized that water was flowing over the length of the five-foot-high bridge before falling to one side and then running underneath it. It was a natural aqueduct. I had never heard of such a thing.

Pigpen Chute is a spot on the Mississagi River, Ontario. Here a lovely campsite overlooks the river. The chute itself is about 10 feet (3m) wide and perhaps 60 feet (20m) long and drops several feet. My teenage granddaughter and grandson found that they could jump in the river just above the chute and let the current carry them to the bottom (wearing PFDs, of course). Then they would run to the top and do it over and over again.

On the Coppermine River, Nunavut, there is a beautiful campsite at Bloody Falls. It is a sand beach with rock outcroppings down by the river. This is where Samuel Hearne's Indian guides massacred a group of local Inuit who were fishing there. At a sharp bend on the Coppermine River, we found slivers of native copper between layers of shale. My paddling partner also found a nugget weighing about a pound. Later he found another where we camped downstream.

Other memories

On a trip down the Attiwapiskat (Ontario), one of our party was a famous NHL hockey player. As we left Pickle Lake, he said, philosophically, that they would know when we were arriving at the town of Attiwapiskat on James Bay. Halfway through the trip, we spent two nights in the mission at Landsdowne House, waiting out some heavy rains. While we were there, a telephone repairman arrived. He thought that he recognized the hockey player, but couldn't figure out how he knew him. He kept asked questions about where the two could have met. Finally as we departed, he realized that he'd seen our compatriot on TV. A week later as we paddled into Attawapiskat, a crowd had gathered on shore near a floatplane. As soon as they spotted us, the whole crowd moved along the shore to where we were headed. Their foreknowledge of our coming was fortunate. A schoolteacher invited us to spend two nights while we waited for the next plane. We were treated to a dinner of lake trout, broiled Canada goose (both purchased from natives for very little), mooseburgers, and a dessert of wild rice pudding. After twenty-four days of dried food, that meal was a real treat.

My wife and I had an opportunity to paddle the Wanganui River in New Zealand with another couple. The banks were composed of pumice, which was so light that chunks that fell into the river floated. This was the only time I have ever encountered floating rocks.

The New Zealand government had built two huts where canoers could sleep and cook. The second of these hostels had been taken over by Maori in a land dispute with the government. A group of Maori offered to carry our things up to the hut. Although I was very apprehensive about staying there, it proved to be a wonderful experience in which we learned much about their culture.

I can remember my colleague pulling the legs of two neophytes by warning them that they should take the paddles into the tent with them to avoid beavers chewing them up at night. At another place he told them to be sure not to take the wrong outlet of a lake, even though lakes rarely have multiple outlets.

Among my favorite recollections are watching the aurora borealis (northern lights) with waves of colored lights wandering through the sky, enjoying brilliant rainbows after a rainstorm, and seeing the sun set well after midnight. In the extreme north, auroras are not easily seen during summer because the sun sets so late, if at all. Clear starry nights are something we don't see in civilization. The early morning mist rising on the river is wonderful for photography, painting, or just watching. Rainbows are more memorable outdoors than when one has waited out the rain in a house or car.

Whenever I see rock paintings made by Indians, my mind wanders to hundreds of years ago when they were made. Interpreting these drawings is like trying to solve a riddle with few clues. I've seen such paintings from Little Missinaibi Lake, on the Bloodvein River, and in the Quetico Park, Ontario.

The diversity of vegetation decreases in the north. There are only a few species of trees prevalent in the boreal forest. The wind north of the tree line is so fierce that it stunts the growth of vegetation. At a lunch break on Schultz Lake on the

Thelon River, Nunavut, my daughter noticed a blueberry plant that was growing so low that a berry lying on the ground was its highest point. The leaves lay flat on the ground.

When I paddled the Winisk River, Ontario, a forest fire burned on one side or the other for over 100 miles. At one point, we camped directly across from active burning. At another spot we walked ashore to within 100 feet of a burning tree. When the flames spread closer and a nearer tree suddenly exploded, we beat a hasty retreat to our canoes, knowing that we would be safe on the water. Our greatest worry about the fire came at a rapids where the fire was actively burning on both shores. Scouting the rapids from shore was impossible and smoke partially obscured our vision from the canoes. Once we committed to the rapids, we found that they were not a serious threat.

We make wilderness canoe trips to get away from all vestiges of civilization. One of the mysteries is why, after a week in the wilderness, we will intentionally paddle to meet another canoeing party. Something inside of us must crave company.

Part of the enjoyment of canoe tripping is pouring over maps in the winter, trying to decide whether a particular river would be navigable and where to go in the spring. The winter also involves drying food, making springerle, and packing them in anticipation of another adventure. A big frustration, however, is getting a group together only to have one of the party drop out at the last moment.

Appendix 1
Interpreting Maps

Estimating the length of a river

The length of a river may be estimated by setting a pair of dividers on the map's scale to a convenient length (e.g. 1 mile or 1 km) and then measure the length by walking the dividers from center of river to center of river. To account for bends, the distance should be multiplied by an appropriate river factor, RF. River factors can be estimated by noting the amplitudes, a, and lengths, L, of bends. The charts on the following page give river factors for different values of a/L.

These charts are based on approximating the river shape as a series of linked arcs of a circle. Using this assumption, $RF = (\theta/2)/\sin(\theta/2)$ and $a/L = [1 - \cos(\theta/2)]/[2\sin(\theta/2)]$ where θ is the angular arc length. In the expressions above θ must be in radians (1 radian = 0.01745 degrees).

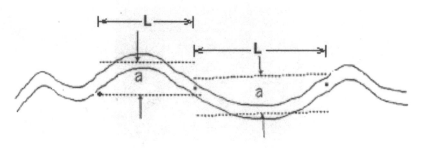

Measuring the length and amplitude of bends.

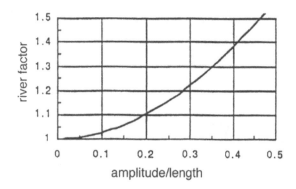

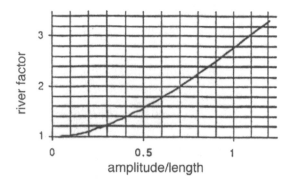

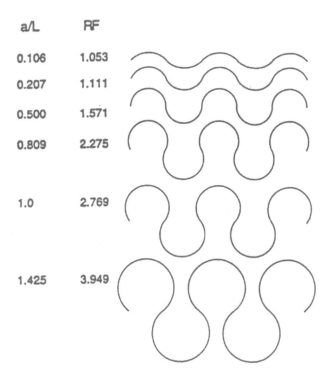

a/L	RF
0.106	1.053
0.207	1.111
0.500	1.571
0.809	2.275
1.0	2.769
1.425	3.949

Another way of estimating the river factor is to make a visual comparison with lines of known river factors. River shapes approximated by circular segments and their corresponding river factors are shown above.

Will there be enough water to paddle?

This is a critical question to ask about small streams. Maps must be carefully examined before making a guess. There are two important factors. One is the area of the watershed and the other is the annual rainfall. The *average* flow rate, F, of a stream in cubic feet /minute should be

$$F = 4.4AR,$$

where A is the area of watershed in square miles, and R is the annual rainfall in inches. If F is expressed in cubic meters per minute, A in square km and R in cm/year,

$$F = 0.96AR.$$

With an annual rainfall of 20 inches and a watershed of 1 square mile, the *average* flow rate is $F = 88$ cu. ft/min. Of interest is the flow rate at the time of canoeing. The river gradient is also important. With a low to moderate slope, a rough rule of thumb for northern Ontario (roughly 20 inches of rain per year) is that one square mile is the minimum watershed to allow a stream to be paddled in May. However, this is only a rough estimate. The unexpected may occur. I have been fooled both ways. Once I had to portage what I expected to paddle because of downed trees. On a trip we expected a three-mile portage from the Dog River watershed to the East Pukaskwa in Ontario. However a beaver had dammed a small creek so we could paddle all but about the last half mile. As a result we called the creek Gofar Creek.

River profiles

Studying the profiles of large rivers will give a clue as to what to expect. Profiles can be constructed by noting the river distance at which each contour is crossed. This is illustrated on the following page. From the plot it is apparent that the gradient in the first half of the trip is about 15 feet per mile, after which it decreases to about 5 feet per mile.

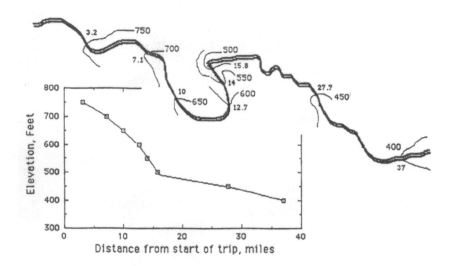

Estimating current

The speed should increase with the gradient and the depth.[1] If the river cross section is approximated as a wide channel of almost constant depth, d, the average velocity, V_{av} is given by $V_{av} = d^{2/3}G^{1/2}/n$ where G is the gradient and n is the Manning coefficient which depends on the nature of the bottom. ($n = 0.02$ for sand, 0.03 for gravel, and 0.04 for rock.)

A profile of the Horton River, Northwest Territories, indicates that the slope is almost constant, except for a steeper region in the canyons. The average slope is G = 350m/600km = .00058. Estimating the average depth, d, as one meter and taking $n = 0.03$ for a gravel bottom, $V_{av} = 0.80$ m/s = 2.9 km/hr. The surface velocity should be about 1.5 times the average velocity or about 4.3 km/hr. This is close to the 3 to 4 km/hr I had observed. A canoe has a very shallow depth, so the surface velocity is more appropriate. This is somewhat greater than the 2 to 3 km/hr that I observed while paddling it. A Manning factor of 0.04 for a rock bottom would give better answers ($V_{av} = 2.2$ km/hr, $V_{surf} = 3.3$ km/hr).

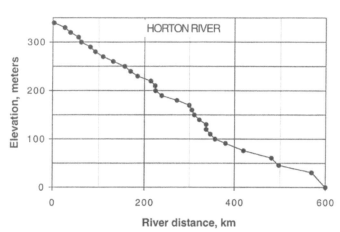

Gradient on the Horton River, Northwest Territories.

---

1   A given river flows faster where it is shallow, but that is because the gradient there is greater. Of course the flow rate of a river is fastest during floods than when it is at normal levels.

Appendix 2
Magnetic Declination

The difference between magnetic north and true north varies with location because the magnetic and true north poles do not coincide. In some parts of Canada, the difference is very large. The magnetic pole is about 1,000 miles south of the true pole, somewhere in Bathurst Island in the Arctic Ocean. Compasses point to magnetic north. Along a line that passes close to Thunder Bay, Ontario, and Ft. Churchill, Manitoba, magnetic and true north coincide. This is called the *agonic* line. East of the agonic line, compasses point west of true north, and west of it they point east of true north. The difference between true and magnetic north is called the magnetic declination. For example the *magnetic declination* is 15° west at Matagami, Quebec, and 37° east at Yellowknife, Northwest Territories. The three figures are charts adapted from Magnetic Declination Chart 1985, Canada Map Office, showing the declinations in 1985. Another figure shows the magnetic declination in Alaska for 1990, taken from the data of *The Magnetic Field in the United States*, 1990, Declination Chart, N.W.

Reddie, 1992 Map GP 1002-D, U.S. Department of the Interior, Geological Survey. Although the declination is continually changing, the rate of change is quite slow, perhaps five minutes per year which is 1 degree in 12 years.

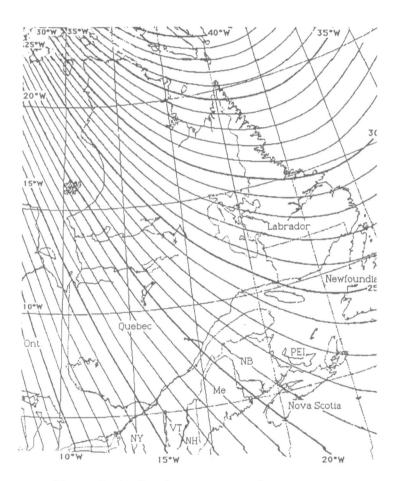

Magnetic declination in eastern Canada, 1985.

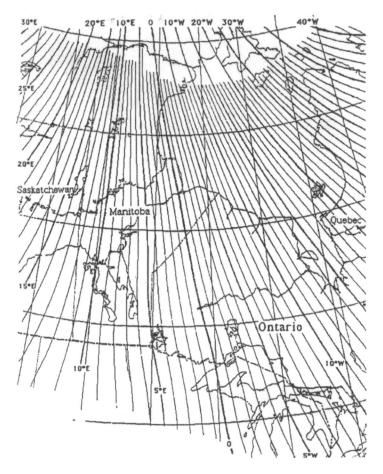

Magnetic declination in central Canada, 1985.

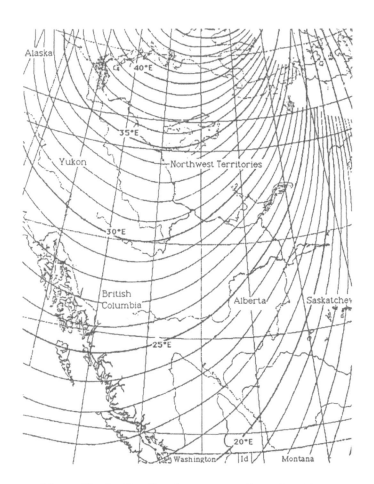

Magnetic declination in western Canada, 1985.

The magnetic data for Alaska are from *The Magnetic Field in the United States*, 1990 Declination Chart, N.W. Reddie, Map GP 1002-D U.S. Department of the Interior, U.S. Geological Survey.

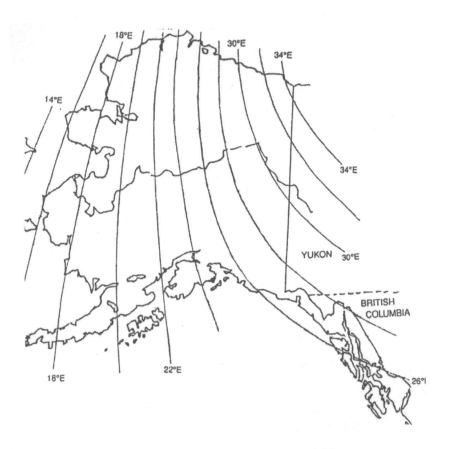

Magnetic declination in Alaska, 1990.

Setting the Compass

Most compasses have an adjustable bar or other indicator, which can be preset at the declination for the region of concern. To use the compass, it should be turned until the needle is aligned with the indicator. The compass directions are then correct. Even when the compass has no indicator, correction can be made by turning the compass until the needle is aligned with the declination.

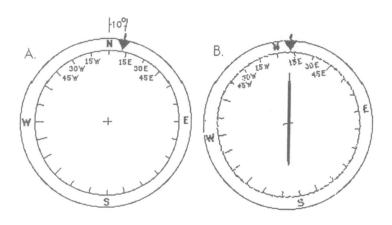

The presence of iron and steel can cause a local disruption of the magnetic field. I remember an occasion on a lake when the party in a companion canoe and I had conferred and agreed on the map where the outlet of a lake was, but we paddled off in different directions. I was looking at the terrain and my compatriot was using his compass. After some shouting, he realized that he was holding his compass over an extra saw blade that he had taped to the bottom of a thwart and this was causing the error.

Appendix 3
Knots

Bowline

The only way I can remember how to tie a bowline is to think of the story my daughter told me. First form a loop (1). One end is a tree trunk, the loop is a rabbit's hole, and the other end is the rabbit. The rabbit comes out of ground (2) and goes around the tree, and back down into his hole (3). This knot is useful in creating a loop that won't self-tighten and is relatively easy to untie.

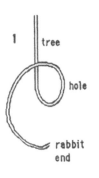
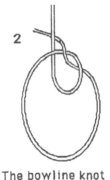

The bowline knot

Fisherman's knot

I had a lot of trouble with this one. More than once I've had a freshly tied lure fly off the line on the first cast. The end of the line should be fed twice around the ring forming a loop (1). Then the free end is wound five to seven times around the long loop (2), fed through the loop, and snipped off (3).

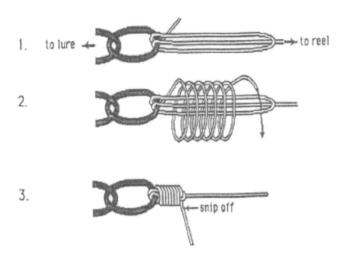

There is another way to tie the fisherman's knot. It involves winding the end five or seven times around a single line (1) feeding the end through the first loop (2) and finally locking the knot by passing the end through the loop just formed (3).

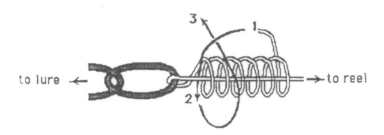

Other useful knots

1. The sheet bend for attaching two ropes even if they have different diameters.

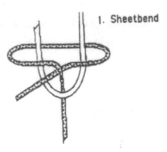

2. The clove hitch for securing canoes to trees.

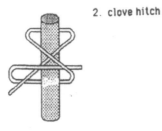

3. The rigger's knot or power cinch for tightening a load.

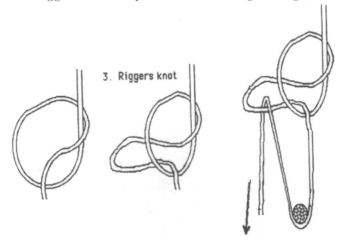

4, The thief's knot for quick release.[1]

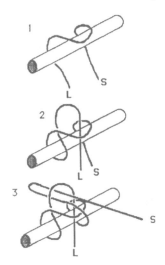

Make a loop and pull it around the fixed bar.

Make a loop in the long end and pull it through the original loop.

Now make a loop in the short end and pull it through the loop in the long end.

Finally, pull the long end until the knot is tight.

The long end can carry a strong force, but the knot can be quickly released by pulling the short end.

---

1   I learned this from a female guide who called it a highwaywoman's knot.

142

Appendix 4
Wilderness Medical Care

First action for injuries

First Aid Primer*

lIf someone is injured, remain calm and patient. Apply the emergency action steps: Check-Call-Care. **Check** the scene to make sure it is safe for you to approach. Then check the victim for consciousness and life-threatening conditions. Someone who has a life-threatening condition, such as not breathing or severe bleeding, requires immediate care by trained responders and may require treatment by medical professionals. **Call** out for help and have someone call 9-1-1 or the local emergency number. There are some steps that you can take, however, to **care** for someone who is hurt until help arrives. For example, administer CPR if the patient does not have a pulse. Check the patient for bleeding or broken bones.

Control Bleeding: Cover the wound with a dressing, and press firmly against the wound (direct pressure). Cover the dressing with

---

* Adapted from redcross.org, 7/2009.

* Adapted from redcross.org, 7/2009.

a roller bandage. If the bleeding does not stop, apply additional dressings and bandages. Provide care for shock.

Care for Shock: Speak calmly and avoid panic. Keep the victim from getting chilled or overheated; cover the patient or put a pad underneath him/her. Elevate the legs about 12 inches (if broken bones are not suspected). Do not give food or drink to the victim. Comfort the person until EMS arrives.

Tend Burns: Stop the burning by cooling the burn with large amounts of water. Cover the burn with dry, clean dressings or cloth.

Care for Injuries to Muscles, Bones and Joints: Rest the injured part. Apply ice or a cold pack to control swelling and reduce pain. Avoid any movement or activity that causes pain. If you must move the patient because the scene is becoming unsafe, try to immobilize the injured part to keep it from moving.

Read more on redcross.org to learn how you can prepare for emergencies.

Hypothermia

Hypothermia (subnormal body temperature) is the most common serious ailment in the bush. One can die of hypothermia even after rescue. The symptoms are slurred speech, clumsiness, and loss of judgment. With severe hypothermia there is a loss of consciousness and a cessation of shivering. Unconsciousness occurs when the body temperature drops to about 86°F (30°C) and death occurs at 82°F (28°C). Immersion in cold water and dampness, aggravated by wind, are the principal direct causes. Contributing factors are often lack of food, dehydration, poor use of clothing, and fatigue. Unnecessary heat loss can result from removal of clothing during a period of rest after sweating, while wearing too much clothing during periods of exercise. Dehydration is more of a problem on canoe trips than one might expect. Sun and wind can cause the body to lose large amounts of water. Without sufficient water, the body can't metabolize food for energy. A yellow color of one's urine indicates dehydration.

Treatment for hypothermia involves getting the patient into dry clothes and into a sleeping bag. Another body in the bag helps. A fire is good but the body should be warmed mainly from the inside. Water and candy should be given if the victim is conscious. A warm drink is good. *Do not drink alcohol!* Do not massage the limbs. Application of warm wet towels will help. It is important to concentrate on warming the body rather the limbs. Warming the limbs can cause an *after drop* (further lowering of body temperature) by the cold blood from the limbs being forced back into the body.

CPR may be necessary. Mouth-to-mouth resuscitation will help warm the lungs and assist breathing. The rescuer's body heat can help warm the victim. Here, use skin-to-skin contact inside a sleeping bag. A book, *Medicine for the Back Country*, by Buck Tilton and Frank Hubbell, K. S. Books, 1999, is a good reference.

First aid kit

A leader of a rescue team in the White Mountains, New Hampshire, says that the most important items in his first aid kit are candy and drinking water for hypothermia, and cloth and tape for splinting. On a canoe trip, candy and water should always available and cloth is part of the normal gear. Other useful items are aspirin, band-aids, and butterfly bandages. Liquid plastic bandages are very good. Other useful items include ace bandages for twisted joints, antibiotics for wounds, and antihistamines for allergies. A needle and thread for suturing could also be added to the list.

Appendix 5
Sunset

Times of sunset

The times of sunset and sunrise vary with latitude, longitude, and time of year. The times of sunset and sunrise in May and August are very different. The summer sun sets very late in northern latitudes. The times of sunset are given in Figure 1. This chart was drawn using data in *The Astronomical Almanac* for 1994 published by The Naval Observatory in Washington D.C. Both sunrise and sunset are defined as the times when the center of the sun is 0.5° below the horizon.

These are true local times and times should be corrected to "legal" time by adding 4 minutes for each degree west of the center of the time zone (or subtracting 4 minutes for each degree east of the center of the time zone. An hour should be added for daylight saving time when applicable. Table I gives the centers of time zones. Figure 2 gives the time zones in Canada.

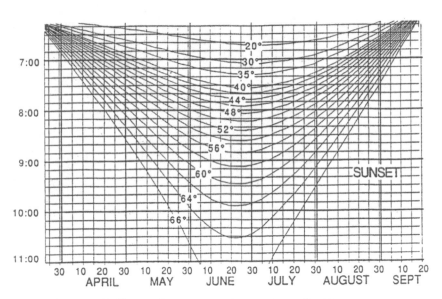

Figure 1. Time of sunset at the center of a time zone.
Numbers indicate latitudes.

Figure 2. Time zones in Canada.

Table 1. Longitudes at centers of time zones

Time zone	Center	Region
Newfoundland	52.5°	Newfoundland
Atlantic	60°	Labrador, PEI, NS, NB, Baffin Is. E of 68°, Que E of 64°
Eastern	75°	Que W of64°, Ont E of 90°, Nunavut between 68° & 85°
Central	90°	Ont W of 90°, Most of Sask, Nunavut between 85° & 102°
Mountain	105°	Alba, northwest Sask, BC east of Rockies. NW Territory
Pacific	120°	BC west of Rockies, Yukon
Alaska	135°	Alaska

Example: Sunset in Nahanni Butte (Latitude = 61°, Longitude = 123°)

For July 1, Figure 2 reads 9:33.

Longitude correction = (123-105)x4 = 72 minutes

Daylight saving correction = 60 minutes

9:33 + 72 min + 60 min = 11:45 pm

Estimating time remaining until sunset

Malo[1] gives the following finger guide for estimating the time remaining before sunset. Face the sun with arms extended and wrists bent so that fingers are horizontal and perpendicular to the arm. With one hand above the other, count the number of fingers between the horizon and the lower edge of the sun. Estimate 15 minutes for each finger. This really works. Average fingers are 7/8-inch thick at their base and are 14 inches from the eyes when the arms are extended. This means they each subtend an angle of about

---

1   John W. Malo, *Wilderness Camping*, Colliers Books, NY 1971.

3.3 degrees. Four fingers subtend 13.3 degrees. This is very nearly equal to the 15°/hour traveled by the sun. This method is only approximate. It doesn't depend on the size of the person. Although larger people have thicker fingers, they also have longer arms.

Estimating azimuth

The differences in azimuth (the angle between a reference plane and a point) between two distant points can be estimated in a similar way by holding fingers vertically at arms length. The angle created by four fingers is approximately 12 to 15°. Remember that the right angle bends are at the wrists rather than the base of the fingers.

Appendix 6
Insects

Black Flies

Black flies and mosquitoes are the bane of the north woods. It is hard to say which is worse. Black flies, often called gnats, are most prevalent in the spring, but springtime varies with location. For many years I canoed with a group that tried to find the one-week window in May between the breakup of the last ice and the start of the black fly season. This timing is very uncertain because the start of the black fly season depends on local temperatures, which vary from year to year and from one location to another. Black flies are inactive until the temperature is above 50°F.

Black flies are very small (about ⅛ inch or 3 mm long). There are a number of varieties of black flies. The most common in the north is *Simulium venustrum*, which are nasty biters. The adult females bite to obtain blood for their eggs. They breed in fast flowing water— unlike mosquitoes, who prefer stagnant water—but may fly seven to ten miles from their breeding grounds. Their life span is four to six weeks, and females bite in the last three weeks of their lives. Males do not bite. They feed on plant nectar and sap. When black flies are present, they number in the thousands.

Black flies tend to bite areas that are not exposed such as up sleeves, under neckbands, at the brim line of hats, in beards, at boot tops, or just under the button lines of shirts. They bite during the day, especially in shaded or partially shaded areas out of the wind. They are most active in the first few hours after sunrise and before sunset. Fortunately black flies disappear after dark no matter how warm it is. They do not bite indoors or at night. If in a tent or inside a head net, they are preoccupied with getting out rather than biting. Reactions to bites vary from one person to the next, causing little irritation in some people to considerable swelling and itching for several days in others. Some people seem to be allergic and suffer great amounts of swelling.

Black flies are attracted by dark-colored clothing, carbon dioxide, perspiration, perfumes, and toiletries. It is advisable to wear light-colored clothing and make sure to avoid entryways by tucking trouser legs into socks, wrapping wrists with tape or rubber bands. The use of head nets, even though they are annoying and limit visibility, is the best way to keep flies off the head. Repellents may keep them from biting, but they don't prevent them from getting into one's mouth, ears, or nose. It is best to wear a head net and button up tightly.

Mosquitoes

Mosquitoes vary in size, with the largest nearly 15 mm (0.6 inch). They fly at 0.9 to 1.6 mph (1.5 to 2.5 km/hr) so one can easily walk away from them. The high-pitched noise of their flight can be very annoying, particularly in a tent at night. Unlike black flies, they do not disappear at night, except when the temperature is below 45° F. Their buzzing inside a tent can be maddening. I have often lain awake at night just wishing they'd bite me and go away so I could get some sleep.

It is the female that bites, or rather sucks blood through her proboscis, to incubate her eggs. Some species lay eggs on moist surfaces (e.g. leaves, mud) and rely on rainwater to stimulate the eggs. Others lay eggs directly on the surface of still water. Their life cycle can vary from fourteen days at 20°C (68°F) to ten days at 25°C (77 °F).

Mosquitoes can sense carbon dioxide and lactic acid up to 100 feet. They are also attracted by certain other chemicals in sweat. Movement, body warmth, and clothing that contrasts against the environment also tend to attract mosquitoes. They are attracted preferentially to some people. It has been said that 10% of the population is highly attractive to mosquitoes.

Their actual bites are painless. The first bite may cause little reaction, but it stimulates the body's immune system so subsequent bites become itchy within a day. Mosquitoes are carriers of several diseases including malaria, dengue fever, encephalitis, and the West Nile virus. Scratching bites increases the itchiness. It has been suggested that with tape applied over a mosquito bite, the itchiness disappears.

Mosquito and black fly seasons vary with location. In southern Canada there is usually a week or so in spring after the ice has gone before the first black flies  appear. But it is hard to judge just when this window will occur because of year-to-year changes. Mosquitoes come out somewhat later. The population of mosquitoes and especially black flies decrease throughout the summer, so late July and August are reasonably bug-free, unless heavy rains have caused a new crop to hatch. The map below is from *Canoe Canada*, N. Nickels, Van Nostrand Reinhold Ltd. 1976, based on data from M. Wood, Biosystems Research Institute, Agriculture Canada, Ottawa.

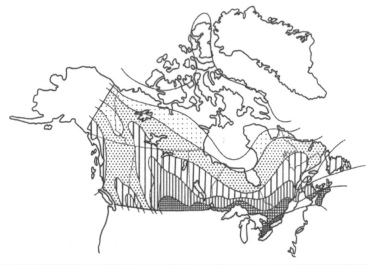

TOTAL SEASONAL PREVALENCE OF MOSQUITOES and BLACK FLIES		PEAK ABUNDANCE	
		Blackflies	Mosquitoes
	1 July - 10 Aug	nil	June 25 - July 30
	21 June - 20 Aug	Aug 1 - 15	June 25 - July 30
	11 June - 31 Aug	July	June 15 - July 30
	1 June - 10 Sept	July	June 10 - July 30
	21 May - 20 Sept	early June - mid July	June 1 - Aug. 10
	11 May - 30 Sept	June	May 24 - Aug 1
	1 May - 10 Oct	mid-May/mid-June nil/southern Ont	May 24 - Aug 1*

several peaks * possible, depending on rains

There is much folklore about what keeps bugs away. Some people claim garlic helps repel black flies. I don't think that works, but I do enjoy garlic. Deet is not always effective. Products containing 35–60% Deet are as effective as those with much higher percentages, and when they do offer protection against biting, it lasts only for a few hours but does not keep black flies far away.

Horseflies and deer flies

Horseflies and deer flies (generically Tabanids) occur in Canada south of the tree line in boreal forests in mid-summer. They are common along beaches, near streams, and at the edges of wooded areas. Horseflies are larger  (3/4 inch to 1¼ inches) than deer flies. Their wings are transparent whereas deer fly wings are boldly colored. Horseflies are mainly attracted to animals, but deer flies often bite humans. Both are attracted by shiny objects, carbon dioxide, and warmth. They are out on warm sunny days when there is little wind. Bites usually occur on the head or around the neck. Their bites are painful, and often exude blood. Creams may help lessen the pain. Some people have allergic reactions to bites.

Bees and wasps

Bees, wasps, hornets, and yellow jackets may attack if they feel their nests are threatened. They may also attack while feeding. They are attracted by perfume and by bright-colored clothing. Their stings are painful and may cause swelling. Swatting yellow jackets crushes their venom sacs and will attract others. Although most people experience only temporary pain and swelling, some have severe allergic reactions. Symptoms include hives, difficulty in breathing, and swollen tongue or face. People who know that they are allergic should carry an emergency kit with an Epipen.

Insect repellents

Insect repellents repel rather than kill insects. Different people swear by their own brand of bug repellent. To my knowledge, they all contain the same active ingredient, Deet. It is an ingredient in most of the commercial repellents, including Off!® and Skin-so-soft®. Its concentration ranges from 4% to nearly 100%. It should not be applied over irritated skin or cuts or abrasions, or near the eyes or mouths of children. Up to 56% of the Deet applied is absorbed into the bloodstream. It may cause a rash, nausea, and irritability. In extreme cases seizures and death have been reported. Products that combine repellents with sunscreen should be avoided because they will likely contain Deet. To reduce absorption, apply Deet-containing products to clothing, not skin.

Several other insect repellents are available. One is 3-aminopropionic acid (N-butyl-N-acetyl), which has been used in Europe for over 20 years without substantial adverse effects. Another is p-methane-3,8 diol which is derived from eucalyptus plants, and for which studies have shown no adverse effects except eye irritation. Citronella and oil of eucalyptus are others. There is no evidence that garlic, bananas, and vitamin B have any repelling effect. A new product, picaridin, has a low oral, dermal, and inhalation toxicity. It is applied to the skin.

I believe that insect repellents should be used sparingly and they are necessary only with severe insect infestations.

Leeches

Leeches are not insects. However many people are repelled by them. You might find them clinging to your body after swimming. They are harmless.

Appendix 7
Waves

Wave length, velocity, and height

The velocity of a wave, V, is related to its wavelength, L, by: V (knots) = 1.34 $\sqrt{L}$ or V (mph) = 1.54 $\sqrt{L}$ or V (ft/sec) = 1.05, where L is in feet. A wave that has a wavelength of 20 feet travels at about 4.7 feet per second, or 6.9 miles per hour. A wavelength of 10 feet indicates a wave velocity of 3.3 feet per second, or 4.9 miles per hour (11 km/hr). Haystacks are standing waves in a river. Although they don't move relative to the shore they do move relative to the water at the water's velocity. The wavelength is the distance between crests. The water velocity through the standing waves can be estimated by determining the wavelength.

For a typical wave, the ratio of the wavelength to height, L/h, is about 30. A fairly steep wave has a ratio of 20. If the wavelength is 20 feet, the height is 1 foot. If L/h reaches about 7, the wave becomes unstable and breaks. This critical ratio is well established for ocean waves created by wind, but it should also hold for standing waves in fresh water.

It is easy to overestimate the height of waves. This is partly because it is difficult to make an accurate estimate directly. Also, in large waves, one views an oncoming wave with a perspective that exaggerates the wave height. The best way to estimate heights of standing waves is to note the wavelength. A large wave for canoers would be $L = 20$ feet (3 m), so with $h/L = 7$, $h =$ about 3 feet (1 m).

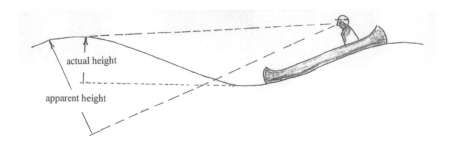

Wind-induced waves

The figure below shows how the wavelength and height depend on wind velocity. These curves are calculated for ocean waves in mid-sea. On lakes the wave height depends on the distance to the windward shore, so the waves won't be as high. A shallow bottom also alters this relationship, creating waves of greater height.

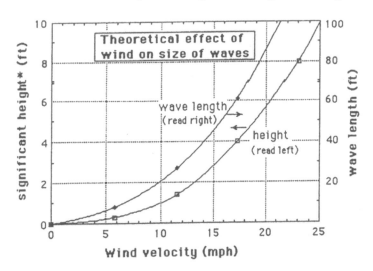

Significant height is the average of the highest ⅓ of the waves.

The water in a wave has a circular motion with a velocity $c_p = \pi h/t$ where h is the wave height, and t is the period (time between crests). The velocity of the wave, V, is given by $V = L/t$ where L is the wavelength.

Waves of different speeds and directions are found in open water. These waves combine with a net effect that the pattern appears irregular. When one spots and follows what appears to be a particularly big wave, it may disappear because it consists of several different waves moving at different speeds. For the ocean as a whole, the following estimates have been made of the frequency of wave heights.

Height (feet)	0-3	3-4	4-7	7-12	12-20	≥ 20
Frequency (%)	20	25	20	15	10	10

Waves and boats

The relationship between the velocity of a wave and its wavelength, $V\,(\text{mph}) = 1.54\,\sqrt{L}$, also holds for waves created by boats. This means that it is impractical to try to power a boat so that $V > 1.54\,\sqrt{L}$ because at that speed the boat has to climb its own wave and the required power increases rapidly. The wake of every boat is at a characteristic angle of $19.5°$ with the direction of travel of the boat. As strange as it may seem, this doesn't change with velocity or style of boat.

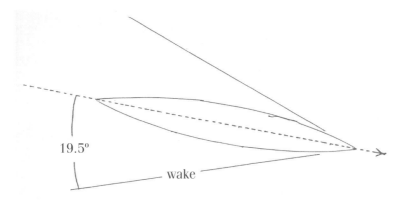

19.5°

wake

Effect of waves

The resistance of waves to the motion of a canoe depends on the ratio of the wavelength to the canoe's length. The greatest resistance occurs when the wavelength is about equal to the length of the canoe. The canoe tends to plunge into each wave and then climb the next. With shorter waves, this effect is lessened. With very long waves, the canoe will gently rise and fall so its motion is similar to that on flat water.

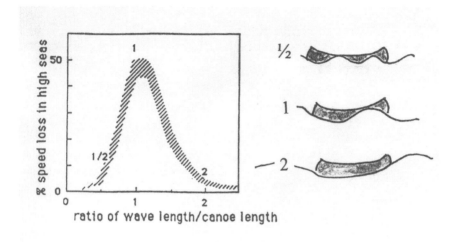

Appendix 8
Mechanics of Canoe Propulsion

Resistance

Naval architects use the term *resistance* for the force required to propel a boat through the water. They divide the resistance into two parts. One is the frictional resistance, R_f, between the boat and the water. This can be calculated from the wetted area, length, and speed. The frictional resistance is given by:

$$R_f = (\rho/2)SV^2C_f,$$

where ρ is the density of water (1.94 lb.sec/ft^4 at 55°F), S is the wetted area in ft^2, V is the velocity in ft/s and C_f is a dimensionless "frictional coefficient" approximately equal to 0.0032 for paddling at 3 mph. Using these values:

$$R_f = 0.0031SV^2.$$

Typically S is about 30–35 ft^2 for a loaded canoe, in which case,

$$R_f = 0.1V^2,$$

where R_f is in pounds and V is in ft/s. At 4.5 ft/s (3 mph) the frictional resistance is one pound.

The residual resistance, R_r, which is the difference between the total resistance and the frictional resistance, is primarily due to energy lost in creating waves and scales with $V/\sqrt{L}$, where L is the wetted length. For $V = 1.5$ ft/s (3 mph) and $L = 16$ ft, $V/\sqrt{L}, = 0.75$ mph /ft$^{1/2}$. In this range the frictional resistance is larger than the residual resistance, though the latter is not negligible. The difference between canoes is largely attributable to differences in residual resistance and this depends strongly on bow shape.

Appendix 9
Animals

Often few wild animals, other than birds, are seen on a canoe trip, so it is a great treat when they are sighted. Some animals live only in forested regions south of the tree line. These include beaver, muskrats, black bear, woodland caribou, and moose. Other animals, like muskoxen, are found only north of the tree line. Most caribou migrate between forests in the winter and tundra in spring and summer. Some animals, including grizzly bears, live in both tundra and forests.

Beaver

The beaver is the animal that affects canoeists the most. They build dams, which create artificial ponds that make it possible to paddle small streams. The wetlands they form are critical to many other species. Their dams and lodges are

made from branches and mud. Some dams are very large. One in Montana was 2,140 feet long, 14 feet high, and 23 feet thick at the base. In civilized areas beaver dams may cause serious damage, flooding roads and blocking culverts. Beaver lodges are built along the shore of their ponds of interwoven sticks. They are large, up to 10 feet tall with wide bases (some up to 20 feet). They have two levels; one for eating and the other for resting. Beavers spend most of their time in the summer storing small branches underwater for the winter by sticking the ends in the mud. Underwater entrances to the lodges provide protection against predators and allow access to stored food in the winter. The only North American animals that gain weight in winter are polar bears, humans, and beavers.

An adult beaver may weigh over 55 pounds and can be 2 feet long, excluding the tail, which is about 10 inches long. Their favorite food is water lilies, but they also eat the bark of trees. Aspen and poplar seem to be favorites. They will fell large aspens to get at the bark of the branches.

When paddling downstream toward a beaver dam, it is best to gather speed and ram it so that the bow rides up on the dam, then get out and, standing on opposite sides of the canoe, pull it over and lower it to the water level below before getting in. Going upstream, the paddlers must get out and lift the canoe over.

Freshly chewed sticks often indicate the presence of beavers in an area. Beavers are territorial and warn other beavers of predators (including humans) by whacking their tails on the water. The noise sounds as if someone has thrown a huge boulder into the water. Several times, I've been awakened at night by an angry beaver slapping its tail on the water. He just wanted us know that he did not approve of where we had camped. Early one morning on the Jackpine River, Ontario, as my wife and I and another couple were eating breakfast, two beavers swam by. One got out on the opposite bank (perhaps 30 feet) away, sat on its haunches, and ate bark from an aspen branch. Its eating method reminded me of the way we eat corn on the cob, working from one end to the other and then rotating the cob to start a new row.

Muskrats

Muskrats live throughout the U.S. and in Canada south of the tree line. Their bodies are 10-14 inches long with a tail 8-11 inches long, and they weigh 20-40 pounds. Muskrats are easily distinguished from other animals by the long, thin tail. They live in marshes and lakes, where they build houses of bulrushes. Muskrats can swim 15 minutes underwater covering up to 300 feet. They are quarrelsome and often fight among themselves.

Otter

Otters live throughout Canada and most of the United States, living in rivers, lakes, and coastal marine areas. They are semi-aquatic with long streamlined bodies. They have short legs with bodies about 3 feet long and thick tapered tails up to 18 inches long. Their life span is usually about eight years. They are excellent swimmers and can stay underwater up to eight minutes. On land they can run 20 miles per hour. They feed mainly on fish and other aquatic life, but will eat eggs and small mammals.

Otters are active from early morning to early evening. They are very playful; they wrestle, dive for rocks, and slide on mud banks. Paddling along a 10-foot-high cliff on

the Severn River, Ontario, I watched one jump into the water next to our canoe and follow the canoe downstream for several hundred feet.

Moose

Moose are the largest members of the deer family. Europeans call them elk. Males (bulls) are easily recognized by their palmate antlers, which may spread six feet. Bulls weigh between 1,200 and 1,600 pounds and females (cows) weigh about 880 pounds. They stand almost six feet high at the shoulders.

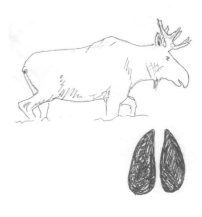

Moose feed on saplings, shrubs, and aquatic plants. They have long legs and can run at speeds up to 34 mph. They frequent marshy areas. In the spring, cows with calves can be very aggressive, as are bulls in the fall rutting season. Collisions with automobiles are very serious.

Foxes

Foxes can be reddish, sandy, brownish-black, or silvery. They are easily recognized by their long, bushy tails. They are about 40 to 45 inches (100 to 112 cm) long including tail. The average life span is 3 to 5 years. They live in burrows dug by other animals. They hunt rabbits, squirrels, mice, birds, and snakes, usually nocturnally and bury some of their food. Foxes warn each other with sharp barks.

Bears

Black bears are usually nocturnal but sometimes active in daylight. They can swim, climb trees, and run up to 30 mph (48 km/hr). They are omnivorous, eating grass, leaves, nuts, fruit, sprouts, fish, eggs, small mammals, and garbage. They do not hibernate, but they sleep much of the winter. They are shy and usually avoid humans, but they will raid garbage cans.

The lower part of the Magpie River, Ontario, is in an area where fumes from an Algoma Steel smelter have killed all of the trees, so berries grow in profusion. On a trip with our children, as we came to a pool with a berry patch, a black bear emerged from the patch and climbed the embankment, calling to a cub that remained in the bushes. After a long delay, the cub came out and followed its mother up the bank. Then we heard more rustling in the bush, and at

Black bear.

first thought it was a second cub, but we wondered why the mother would abandon a cub. Then all of a sudden, an otter emerged from the berry patch, leaping toward us into the water, swimming under our canoes before surfacing. When it started hissing, we realized that it too had a cub in the berry patch. The cub came out on a log, saw us, and retreated again into the bushes. It finally came out only after repeated beckoning from its mother.

We camped not far from there, but on the opposite side of the river. We were somewhat concerned because of bear tracks on the shore. Since all trees had died, we couldn't haul our packs out of reach of bears, so we just pitched our tents far from the food packs. The next morning we did see a bear on the hillside above us, slowly eating his way down the hill toward us. When he saw us, he changed directions. We watched him gradually work his way back up the hill. Once at the top, he saw something that made him gallop at full speed along the ridge. The only thing I can think of to explain his behavior is that he saw his mother, who had recently rejected him in order to raise another cub.

Grizzly bear.

Grizzly bears are found in British Columbia, Alberta, Yukon, Northwest Territories, Nunavut, Alaska, Idaho, Wyoming, Washington, and Montana. They feed on roots, berries, plant bulbs, pine nuts, rodents, and fish. They are known for their appetite for salmon. They sometimes raid caches of nuts stored by squirrels and can smell carrion from long distances. They may prey on live moose, mountain sheep, and mountain goats, especially calves.

Grizzlies can be recognized by their concave, dish-like faces and humped shoulders. Their colors range from blond to dark brown or black. Their front tracks are 6-8 inches long excluding heel and 7-9 inches wide. The hind tracks are 12-16 inches long and 8-10.5 inches wide.

Grizzlies are active in early morning and evening hours. Grizzlies usually flee at first sense of humans—but not always. They are far more dangerous than black bears. They reach sexual maturity at 4-5 years and are fully grown by 8-10 years. Adult females weigh 270-770 pounds; males weigh 330-1150 pounds. I've seen grizzlies only on the Thelon and Burnside (Nunavut); Mountain, Nahanni, and Keele rivers(Northwest Territories). One swam across the Mountain

River between the two lead canoes and the following two. It was so terrified by us that it disappeared as fast as it could.

On the Burnside, as we ate lunch, we saw a grizzly with two cubs in the far distance. Initially we were hoping that they would come closer so we could get a better view. However, we became apprehensive when they finally did come closer. When they were about 50 yards away, we were beating on pots and waving raised paddles to ward them off. Finally, the mother bear stood up on her haunches to get a better view of us, then dropped to all fours, and sauntered off.

Caribou

Caribou belong to the deer family. They eat moss, lichen, and green vegetation. Northern caribou winter in forests but migrate north in spring to calve. They travel in large herds. Their babies can walk an hour after birth. Hollow hair, which is very insulating, gives buoyancy  when swimming. Most females have antlers. Adult bulls average 350-400 pounds and females average 175-225 pounds. The average age of a caribou is about 4 years. Herds move constantly to avoid flies and mosquitoes, which plague the animals, to find food and avoid predators. Wolves, grizzly bears, and eagles kill many young.

Their principal foods are willow leaves, sedges, and various tundra plants. In the fall they eat lichen and small shrubs. Their migrations are governed by weather. They travel long distances; 400 miles is common. They will use the same migration routes for years, but may suddenly change routes.

Woodland caribou live in the boreal forests. They need to be at least 10 miles from the nearest road so they are being threatened by logging roads. Woodland caribou are slightly smaller than the northern caribou. They are solitary or occur in very small groups. Their average age is six years.

Muskoxen

Muskoxen are herbaceous herd animals that gather in packs of 10-20 animals and feed on grass and willows. They live north of the tree line. When threatened, they form a circle with calves in the center. This habit nearly led to their extinction because they would maintain the circle instead of fleeing while hunters shot them. In early 1900s

muskoxen were almost extinct because of hunting for meat and fur. Today, muskoxen are protected by law and they number about 60,000.

A muskox is on the average 4 feet tall and weighs 440-900 pounds. Both males and females have horns. Their soft, highly insulating (8 times more insulating than wool) underwool, qiviut, is shed in the spring. The Inuit collect it for sweaters and scarves. Muskox hooves spread, allowing them to walk on snow, yet are sharp enough to dig for grub. A cow has its first calves at about three years and gives birth every other year.

Wolves

Wolves are often brown or gray. They are very social and live in packs. They eat fish, lemmings, birds, foxes, and squirrels. During the caribou migrations they form packs to hunt caribou. A pack sets ambushes and usually prey on sick animals. If a deer turns and fights, they may try to find an easier prey. Top speed for wolves is 30-35 mph. Their tracks are 4-5 inches long with a stride of 26-30 inches. Each pack has one alpha female who has an average of seven pups. The whole pack helps feed the pups. One member of the pack will stay awake, acting as a guard. The range of a pack may be as great as 250 miles (350 km). They use urine to mark their territory.

Wolves are skittish. I've seen wolves only rarely, but I'm sure that many wolves have seen me. Once as I walked on an old logging road, I saw the prints of a wolf going in the opposite direction. On returning I saw prints on top of mine. The wolf had apparently seen or heard me coming, gone into the bushes until I had passed, and then resumed walking on the road. Another time on the Thelon River, Nunavut, I watched a wolf trail a sickly caribou, waiting for it to tire.

Wolverines

Wolverines are the largest members of the weasel family. They are very fierce for their size (about the size of a black bear cub). Their fur is used for trimming the hoods of parkas. A wolverine's territory may be as large as 200 square miles. Their large feet help them travel on top of the snow. They ambush their prey. They are very elusive and rarely seen. I was fortunate enough to get a quick look at one on the Mountain River.

Squirrels

The northern squirrels' formal name is the Richardson Ground Squirrels, but the Inuit call them "sic sics." Sometimes they are called gophers, but they are not gophers. Adults are about a foot long. They live in colonies and make underground dens with lots of tunnels. They are often seen standing erect. They eat tundra plants, seeds, fruit in spring and summer, and they hibernate in winter.

Other animals

Other animals of the north include lynxes, porcupines, badgers, and skunks, which live south of the tree line. Lynxes are about 3 feet long and weigh about 25 pounds and are now a protected species.

Appendix 10
Glossary of Canoeing Terms

ait A small island in a river.

beam The maximum width of the canoe. The *waterline beam* is the maximum width at the waterline.

bent shaft A paddle in which the shaft is angled to the blade.

black fly A small flying insect half the size of a housefly; they are everywhere in the north during daylight making life miserable in the spring and summer.

blaze A mark to indicate a portage trail. It may be on a tree trunk (axe blaze) or a broken twig (twig blaze).

boil Region of upwelling water in which there is a mixed current.

bow The front end of a canoe.

bow rudder A risky steering maneuver made from the bow by thrusting the blade of the paddle at an angle across the bow.

brace A paddle position for achieving stability. The paddle is vertical in the *high brace* and almost horizontal in the *low brace.*

braided river   A river with many intersecting channels, which from the air looks like braided hair.

breakout   An abrupt turn that occurs as the bow enters an eddy, arresting its motion while the current swings the stern around, often leading to a capsize.

cagoule   A pull-over piece of rain gear with a hood; it is long enough to cover the knees. A three-quarter-length rain parka.

cairn   A pile of stones sometimes marking a trail.

canot du maitre   A very large (35-foot) freight canoe used on the Great Lakes by the voyageurs in the fur trade.

canot du Nord   Smaller (25-foot) canoe used in the fur trade west of the Great Lakes.

carry   Portage.

chain   Some portages are measured in chains (66 feet), which is the length of a cricket pitch.

chute   A constricted channel of water.

cross draw   A draw executed by the bow paddler without changing grip on the handle.

D-ring   A ring in the shape of the letter D to which a strap can be fastened. D-rings are used on packs and on the bottom of the canoe for lashing gear.

dead head   A log in the river, one end of which is sunken and the other above water.

draft   The depth of water that a canoe needs to float.

draw   A paddling stroke used in either bow or stern in which the paddle blade is parallel to the canoe and pulled toward the canoe. Used for steering to change direction.

Duluth pack   A large canvas knapsack with a single pocket equipped with a tumpline.

eddy	A place in a river where the current is in the opposite direction from the main flow, often behind a large rock or island, along shore or behind bridge abutments.
eddy out	To pull into an eddy out of the current. Also to come to shore where there is no actual eddy but the different water velocity slows the bow allowing the stern to swing downstream.
feathering	Twisting of the paddle blade parallel to the water on the return stroke above water to minimize air resistance.
ferry	A maneuver used to cross a river in which the canoe is angled to the current and paddled upstream. Used to minimize downstream drift. In the *back ferry*, the canoe is paddled backward while facing downstream and angled to the current.
freeboard	The distance between the gunwales and the water.
giardia	A severe intestinal disease caught from drinking water infected by (often, beaver) excrement.
gunnel	Alternative spelling of gunwale.
gunwale	The upper edge of the side of a canoe; the strip of plastic, wood or aluminum running from bow to stern along the side.
haystacks	High standing waves in a fast section of river, horses.
horses	Also white horses. Standing waves with breaking crests.
hypothermia	A severe reduction of body temperature leading to loss of judgment, unconsciousness, and even death.
inwale	The inboard portion of the gunwale.

J-stoke	The normal stroke of the stern paddler at the end of which there is an outward thrust to turn the canoe enough to compensate for the turning action of the bow paddler.
keel	A strip along the center bottom of the canoe usually extending the full length. The keel stiffens the bottom and helps keep the canoe on a straight course.
keeper	A backwater whirlpool that "keeps" things.
lee	Direction opposite to the wind. Protection from the wind offered by objects on the shore.
lining	The use of painters to guide an unoccupied canoe downstream from shore.
outwale	The outboard portion of the gunwale.
painter	Rope line attached to the bow of a canoe. Canoes often have stern painters as well.
pear handle	The handle of a canoe paddle that roughly resembles a pear.
PFD	Personal flotation device or life jacket.
piéce	A 90-pound bundle of furs transported by the voyageurs.
poling	Propelling a canoe by pushing a long pole against the lake or river bottom.
portage	To carry a canoe and cargo overland between navigable waters. Also the act of carrying and the trail on which the carry is made.
pry	A steering maneuver in which the paddle blade is forced outward using the gunwale as a fulcrum.
pull over	Moving the canoe, without unloading, a short distance around a fall or other obstacle.
rib	The reinforcing member of a canoe, perpendicular to the keel. Used mainly on canvas-and-wood or aluminum canoes.

riffle	Shallow rapid with small waves.
river factor	The ratio of the actual to straight-line distances along a river.
river right	The right side of the river facing downstream. Similarly, river left is the left side of the river facing downstream.
rock garden	A section of river filled with rocks, often with insufficient water for paddling.
rocker bottom	A curved keel line that is lower in the middle than at the ends.
run	Shoot a rapid.
shoe	A steel cup fastened to the end of a pole used to pole a canoe.
skid plate	A reinforcement of bow or stern.
snag	A tree or part of a tree anchored fast to the bottom forming a hazard to progress.
snye	A minor river channel, especially on a braided river.
stern	The rear of the canoe.
swamp	To fill a canoe with water.
sweeper	A fallen tree trunk or branch extending outward from the shore so that it is a dangerous obstruction to passage. Also the last canoe in a guided party that can assist others in trouble.
T-handle	A style of paddle handle formed by a small piece perpendicular to the shank.
throw bag	A bag filled with rope that will play out as the bag is thrown. Used in rescues.
thwart	A cross member extending from one gunwale to the other, which spreads and stiffens the hull.

tie-down	A D-ring or other device to which gear can be secured.
tongue	Fast-moving water forming a V at the start of a rapid.
tracking	Upstream lining; pulling a canoe upstream either from shore or by wading.
tumblehome	Half of the horizontal distance by which the maximum hull width exceeds the distance between gunwales.
tumpline	A leather strap around the forehead to help support a pack on one's back.
upset	Tilting of the canoe at least 90° so water fills the canoe.
V-bottom	V-shaped cross section of the hull.
Voyageur	A person, usually French-Canadian, who transported goods and furs by canoe to and from trading posts.
wanigan	A large box for carrying food and kitchen supplies.

Appendix 11
References

A Paddler's Guide to the Rivers of Ontario and Quebec, Kevin Callan, The Boston Mills Press, 2003.

Canoeing Canada, Nick Nickels, Van Nostrand and Reinhold, 1976.

Canoeing Canada's Northwest Territories, Mary McCreadie, Canadian Recreational Canoe Association, 1995.

Canoeing Ontario's Rivers, Ron Reid and Janet Grand, Douglas and McIntyre, 1985.

Expedition Canoeing, 3rd Ed., Cliff Jacobson, Globe Pequot Press, 2001.

Freshwater Saga: Memoirs of a Lifetime of Wilderness Canoeing, Eric W. Morse, University of Toronto, 1987.

From Reindeer Lake to Eskimo Point, Peter Kazaks, Natural Heritage/Natural History, Inc. 2003.

How to Shit in the Woods, Kathleen Meyer, 10-Speed Press, 1989.

Medicine for Backcountry, Buck Tilton and Frank Hubbell, ICS Books, 1990.

Muskeg, Mosquitoes, and Moose, Joyce A. Stone, Wilderness Adventure Books, 1992.

Nutritional Value of Foods, C.F. Adams and Martha Richardson, Science and Education Administration, U.S. Department of Agriculture, 1978 (for sale Superintendent of Documents U.S. Government Printing Office, Washington D.C. 20402 Stock # 001-000-03481-9).

The Canoe Guide's Handbook, Gil Gilpatrick, DeLorme Publishing Co., 1981.

The Complete Wilderness Paddler, J. W. Davidson and John Rugge, A. A. Knoff, 1976.

The Open Canoe, Bill Riviere, Little Brown, 1985.

Wilderness Camping, John W. Malo, Colliers Books, NY, 1971.

Wilderness Survival Handbook, Alan Fry, 1996.